MAKING INDIAN BOWS AND ARROWS . . . THE OLD WAY

by
Douglas Spotted Eagle

Eagle's View Publishing Edition

Eagle's View Publishing Company
6756 North Fork Road
Liberty, Utah 84310

ISBN 0-943604-21-4

DEDICATION
To Poppa Longbow, Josh, Amanda and my buffalo
brother who is with me always.

15 14 13 12 11 10 9 8 7

TABLE OF CONTENTS

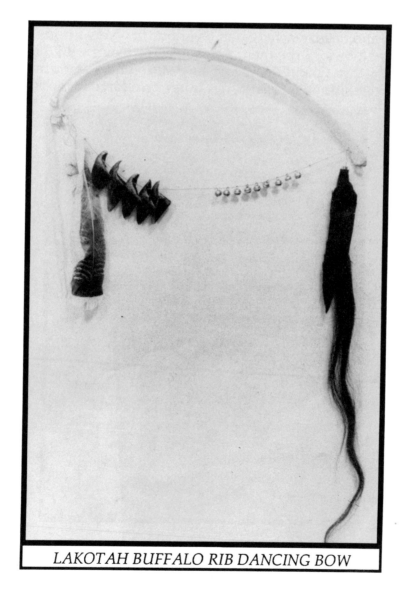

LAKOTAH BUFFALO RIB DANCING BOW

ABOUT THE AUTHOR

Doug Spotted Eagle, shown wearing 1840 Lakotah clothing, is a noted authority on the Plains Indian culture. He and his wife restore and replicate Plains artifacts for museums and private collections.

Spotted Eagle's investigation of Native American bows began after a motorcycle accident left his left arm crippled. He was fortunate in finding a few old-time bowyers who were willing to share their time and talent teaching him the old ways of making bows. Since then, he has become well known throughout the Western states for his hunting skill and for his bows and arrows. He has successfully hunted buffalo, elk, deer, and pheasant with a primitive bow, as well as winning many primitive archery competitions. In 1987, he was named the Primitive Archer of the Year. Doug's talent for making bows is widely acknowledged, yet he is even better known for his skill in making arrows from natural materials and in 1987, he wrote a booklet on how to make arrows. The success of the arrow booklet, and the help of various bowyers throughout the country, enabled him to write this book on making, shooting and understanding Native American bows, an effort of which he is justifiably proud.

ACKNOWLEDGEMENTS

When a couple of friends jokingly suggested that I write this book, I did not take them very seriously. After a summer of rendezvous where I saw many friends walking around camp with bows that I had made, the idea started to gnaw at my brain. I began to put together photos and notes that I had acquired over the years, and gathered additional material from many old friends working in museums around the country. I even made some new friends. All of this information was compiled, written, re-written, and edited to create this book.

No author can say "I wrote this all by myself" and be truthful, because no man can become all things. I wish to pay tribute to all those who helped me "become all things" particularly: "Poppa" Longbow Safford, who has forgotten more about making old Indian bows than most will ever know; Dr. Charles Grayson, who has built and restored bows for many museums including the Smithsonian; and, T. M. Hamilton, the author of Native American Bows, who has graciously permitted me to reprint charts from his bible of Indian archery. Fred Bear cannot be forgotten; his knowledge and wisdom will be passed down through the ages. Unfortunately, he will never see this book as he died during the publication process. These men are the last of the old-time bowyers, and we can only hope that this great art is not lost when they are gone. The information they have so willingly shared will help keep this tradition alive. I wish to thank them all for the countless hours of articulate instruction and phone calls. Much of the research would not have been possible without them.

Archie Fire, Lloyd Topsky, Gary Prettypaint, Mark Wolfchild, Jim Bilagody and Luther American Horse - thank you all for sweating with and for me; the truth did come out. I also want to thank the following for the use of their equipment: Chad Rindlisbacher of Red Hawk Trading for his Cheyenne bow and quiver (every bow in this book has been made by myself except for his outstanding work of art); Terry Rosenlund for his Crow otter case and quiver; and, George Knowlden for his Nez Perce/Crow bow case and quiver. In addition, I wish to thank Richard Conn, curator of Indian Collections at the Denver Art Museum for his assistance; Bill Holm, curator of the Thomas Burke Memorial Museum in Washington, and a bowyer of great skill, for his help; Stanley Honour, for his words of wisdom at rendezvous many years ago; and, Dan Quillian, who is the only living expert on traditional longbows. His knowledge begins where that of most bowyers' ends.

Not to be forgotten, are Jim and Virginia Glendenning and everyone else at Woods Unusual, who pushed my arrow publication and forced me to get this book done before the year 2000. They also allowed me to reprint descriptions and charts from Stemmlers Archery Workshop which greatly clarify certain concepts for the reader. Linda and Shirley Dee for the moral support offered and taken; Doug Collins, who gave his life that this book may live; John Zaker, whose wit, wisdom, and cover photo appear in this book; Beth Denner shot the first arrows I made, and then lied about how good they were, and then out-shot me with them. Doug Walker and the staff at Western Bowhunter gave me good advice; Jim Morrell was very patient, letting me take pictures again and again of the bows I had made; Carey Beckstead and Dave Jager took time to do research and read my manuscript, making sure there were few errors.

I also cannot forget Lyn Wallentine, whose artistic talents graced the illustrations, in the first edition, and some of the photos in this volume, and who put up with me and the late hours I spent at the typewriter trying to spell correctly. She has been a major asset to this project, and it could not have been completed without her inspiration and assistance. My thanks and love to my son and daughter, who spent countless hours understanding the absence of Daddy.

Although I am solely responsible for the contents of this book, for advice and corrections, included in the Eagle's View Edition, I would like to sincerely thank Denise Knight. The number of hours that she devoted to making this a better book are very much appreciated.

Also, my thanks to Ralph L. (Smitty) Smith for the graphics work in this edition, to Brenda Martin for proofing the new edition, and to my publisher and editor, Monte Smith.

Last, but not least, I wish to thank my Grandfather, who gave me a love for the traditions and histories of life and my parents and friends, too numerous to mention, for standing by when help was needed.

Grandfather, in a humble way I thank you for the opportunity to share what little I may with others who also have a love of the old ways. Aho...

INTRODUCTION

ARCHERY . . . Just the word seems to invoke awe in the minds and hearts of men. Nearly every recorded culture has used the bow and arrow to civilize, feed, protect, and entertain. It seems odd, even magical, that a staff of wood and a few sticks could bring a man to the height of glory. Man has equated the bow with love and hate, death and life, and, with the Archer in the heavens, sometimes as a god. Perhaps Thompson said it best in his book, *The Witchery of Archery*, when he wrote, "so long as the new moon returns in heaven a bent, beautiful bow, so long will the fascination of archery keep the hearts of men."

The Indians of the North American continent more than likely did not look upon the bow as a romantic artifact of their culture, but they did use the bow to conquer, feed, protect, and survive. Perhaps it is because their history is so intertwined with our own that Native American archery is so entrancing. Perhaps, it is because the Indian fought our ancestors with the arrow, and often won.

This book is not an attempt to explain why historians, buckskinners, and Scouters of today are addicted to Indian archery; rather, it is a small attempt at providing information for this hunger to feed upon. I hope it will expand the knowledge and curiosity of those who read it.

Native American archery is as different from modern or European archery as white is from black. It has its own mysticism and power to hold the heart captive. The culture of the Plains people revolved around the bow and the buffalo. Many times, arrows and/or bows were used in religious ceremonies, or were represented in those ceremonies. The Cheyenne people have been known to give their lives to retain possession of their Sacred Arrows.

As is typical of subjective topics, every historian, curator, anthropologist, or amateur ethnologist has presented opinions about the Indian and the bow and they have not always agreed. I too, have something to say; my purpose is not controversy, but understanding and acceptance. Many bowyers have different points of view on Indian methods and practices regarding bow making and arrowsmithing. I have presented my own perspective in this book as well as the views of others, with whom I may agree or disagree. I feel a project is incomplete unless all viewpoints are considered. Many of the topics presented are contrary to currently accepted opinions, and for this I make no apology. There is a list of archery terms in the back of this book which may be referred to as needed.

Until T. M. Hamilton published his study of Native American bows there were no documents on Indian archery for the bowyer to study. Reginald Laubin's book presented many ideas, most of them valid, and he promoted Indian archery more than had been done previously in this century. Dr. Pope's studies in the 1920s, concluded that Indian bows were "good for their savage means," but Pope was a longbowman and apparently did not understand the differences in cultures and application. Many have called Pope the contemporary Father of Indian Archery, but I wish to point out that the results of the tests he so diligently performed with Indian bows were compromised because they were done with weapons that were a century old and had been stored in heated attics. Some had been left strung for many years; a few were even strung backwards. Pope tells us that the bows performed poorly, having a best cast of 210 yards, yet bows made by myself and others have far surpassed that mark. Our primitive archery club frequently *clout* shoots at distances of 225

1

yards. I once saw a short bow of Osage orange wood (made by Stan Honour of Denver) shoot an eighteen inch arrow over 400 yards.

I think many people love the longbow because of their ease of manufacture, and the "sweetness" of their draw. Traditionally longbows have a feel that is unlike any other bow. They shoot neither better nor worse than the Indian short bows - only differently.

Today, few Indians if any, have ever shot a bow. At Crow Fair (Montana), I met an old Arapaho man who told me about his grandfather making bows for young men in the Tribe. This man thought his grandfather had been born "around 1900," so it is entirely possible that the methods he described were correct. At some of the archery demonstrations where I have performed, young Indian children have come up and tried the old style bows; they like them, but cannot relate them to anything familiar.

The Indian way of life has disappeared due to the white man's laws and the reservation system. Fortunately, knowledge of many of the old ways has been retained by many Indian people who have a desire to incorporate them into their lives. You can never go back to what was, but you can bring "what was" forward and make today a better day.

I did not write this book to promote myself as a great hunter, competitor, or bowyer; I wrote it because I hope this book will benefit people involved in these activities. I have been a successful hunter, with a primitive bow, as well as a *paper-puncher*. These activities have opened up an entire world of Native American culture that I did not know existed, and the bow allowed me to accomplish a goal that most men can only dream about. My wife has recently developed a love for the sport as well. I mention her as this work would not have been possible without her help. Few spouses would have put up with wood shavings in the carpet, raw hides in the basement, brains and hooves on the stove, and her crock-pot full of glue. She has always encouraged these things and has never discouraged me. Thanks to her, my life is full and fun. She granted me the opportunity to produce this book, and I thank her for it.

WOODS AND TOOLS

Before we can begin to work on a bow, we have to acquire some tools and a bit of wood.

Getting the tools is easy, especially if you intend to make the bows using only traditional tools. This method requires a knife, wood or antler wedges, sandstone, obsidian, and an axe or hatchet. A rough file will help if you don't mind being a little less than a purist.

If you wish to make the bow with more efficient tools than a stone, yet do not want to go completely modern, you will need the following: a band or table saw, draw knife, shoemakers file, pocket plane, small plane, and a ruler with pencil. There are many other tools you can use, but these are the essentials.

After deciding the method you will use to make your bow, you must choose the wood with which you want to work. Rather than listing all the woods used to make bows, suffice it to say that any wood, except conifer wood is acceptable. The exception to this rule is the Douglas fir (a conifer) which has been used in bows, but which I have not personally tried.

Some woods do make better bows than others: Ash, hickory, black locust, apitong, choke cherry, birch, juniper (Mormon cedar), white oak, lemon wood, Osage orange (also known as hedge apple or Bois d'arc), red cedar, mountain mahogany, apple, yew, and iron wood all make excellent bows. Golden oak, willow, and Chinese elm do not make good bows.

✠ ✠ ✠

This book deals with Native American bows west of the Mississippi River, so I will discuss woods that make good short bows. By "short," I mean those less than fifty-four inches in length. The woods listed above, except lemon wood and white oak, all work well. Lemon wood and white oak are for the longbowman and are too brash or brittle for good short bows.

For the first time bowyer, hickory and ash are excellent choices. They are readily available and both are forgiving of minor mistakes.

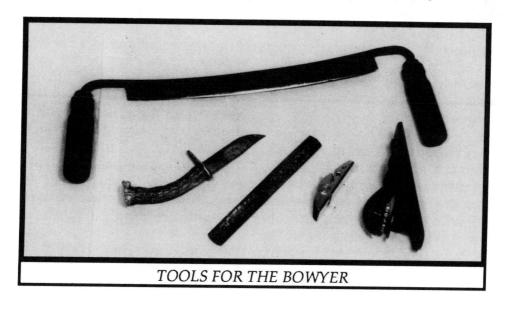

TOOLS FOR THE BOWYER

OSAGE ORANGE LOG

Black locust and choke cherry are good intermediate choices, while Osage orange or yew are best left for the experienced bowyer. This is because Osage orange and yew are the hardest woods to work with. Osage orange is also hard to locate in any quantity and, if you make a mistake, it could be a very expensive error.

Although some bowyers feel Osage orange is a far superior bow wood, the Indians do not appear to have felt the same way. Hickory and ash are by far the most common woods from which Indian bows were made. Of one hundred Plains bows recently examined, only twelve were of Osage orange; thirty-nine were hickory, sixteen were ash, seven were horn, and the balance were made from other assorted wood. If the Indians had felt Osage was the best wood, they could have obtained it through trade; *Osage orange* obtained its name from its unusual color and because the Osage and Kiowa used it as a trade item. Also, the Lakotah bands of the Sioux Nation were well-known archers, but they did not use Osage wood. True, Osage is quicker and has more *snap* if worked properly, but it is a poor choice for the first time bowyer.

Wood can be found and identified in many odd places. For instance, an old farm in Alabama was fenced entirely with Osage, or "hedge apple," and hickory. Of course, the property was re-fenced with red cedar and the old "deadwood" hauled away for better uses. The point is, you should keep an eye out for good straight limbless trunks and branches. The fence or shed down the road may hold hidden treasures. Find out, if you can.

If you take your wood from a tree, cut it after the first frost; mid-January is best. When possible, use a saw instead of an axe as it is much easier to treat the ends of a clean cut log than the ends of one that is rough. Cut your log from a four to six inch diameter tree and make it approximately sixty inches in length.

Once you cut your wood, leave the bark on the trunk and paint the ends of the log thoroughly with wax or latex paint. This allows the log to dry from the outside-in, as opposed to drying from the inside-out. Put your wood away in a warm (not hot), dry place to season for at least three months. If you want to make your stave (or *bow blank*) the Indian way, then skip the seasoning stage at this point and continue. The Turks allow their bow woods to dry for at least five years. **Note:** When possible, cut more than one log in case of foul wood. You will also have more wood if you wish to make more bows.

After the wood is aged, or not aged (the Indian fashion), the log needs to be split into staves. You will need wood or antler wedges and a maul. The logs you have cut will have splits in them. Put the wedges in these cracks and proceed to split the staves from the log. Follow the grain of the wood and you will get two to three, two inch by one and one-half inch staves out of the log. About half of these will make bows, so expect to ruin a stave or two during a first-time project.

Quite often an Indian either did not want to cut down a tree or did not have the necessary tools. Instead, he would find a tree with splits in the wood and cut the staves directly from the trunk. Placing the wedges into the splits on the tree, he would cut a notch at the top of the trunk, and one at the bottom; the distance between the notches being the length of the bow. Then he would pound out the stave by alternately hitting the wedges until the stick fell free. The stave was then seasoned by rubbing fat over the entire bow and hanging it in the top of the lodge in the fire's smoke. It was kept there for a week or two and then the bow was worked into shape. The stave was always cut during the cold months which solved the moisture problem.

✠ ✠ ✠

After reading the above on how to prepare and season a stave, you may wish to find a wood house or archery supply shop that will sell you

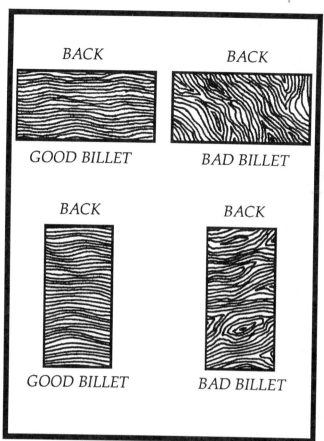

BACK   BACK

GOOD BILLET   BAD BILLET

BACK   BACK

GOOD BILLET   BAD BILLET

CLOSE-UP OF BARK AND GROWTH RINGS

a pre-cut, pre-seasoned billet of wood. The thing to remember is that the wood must be air dried, not kiln dried. Some shops will tell you they are the same process and that it doesn't make a difference. Do not believe this, as it may mean the difference between a good bow or a broken one. Kiln dried wood has air pockets

that develop during the drying stage and it will be brash or brittle. There are companies that specialize in air-dried woods.

When choosing a stave or billet, look at the grain on both ends of the wood. It should be fairly straight and free of twists between the ends. A bit of grain variance is not a problem unless you are working with Osage orange. Osage must be worked within one growth ring on the back of the bow. The stave or billet you choose must be fairly free of knots. Some bowyers say that a good bow cannot have any knots in it, but I disagree as the bow that killed my first buffalo has a knot that measures one by three-fourths of an inch; it also has a slight twist to the grain.

A bowyer can work around twists if he is conscious of the pattern of the grain. Some bowyers have the absurd notion that the grain must be flawless, but this is really an excuse either for being afraid of a difficult stave, or simply for being a poor bowyer.

5

Remember, many woods are forgiving. Indian bowyers were fairly critical of their woods, but not to the extent that some bowyers are today. Be critical, but see minor problems with the wood as a challenge, not as an obstacle. Keep in mind that wood is a natural material and is rarely perfect in form.

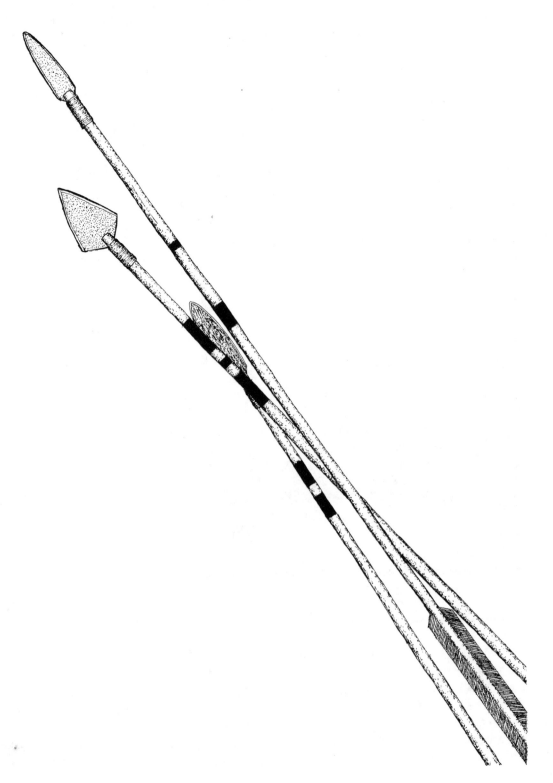

BOW STYLES

What is a bow? This may seem like a silly question, but most people would be surprised at the number of times I am asked how a bow works. A bow is basically two limbs acting as springs that are kept in tension by a string. When the string is drawn back, energy is created and stored in the limbs. When the string is released, the energy is released and transferred to the arrow. If an arrow is not present, the energy cannot be transferred and must be released through the limbs. In such a case, the limbs may approach a negative bend, after passing their normal relaxed position, and can shatter or crack, depending on the strength of the bow. For this reason a bow is never drawn and quickly released when there is no arrow to the string; to do so is known as *dry firing*.

The distance an arrow travels upon release is known as *cast* and quite often a bow's ability is judged by the amount of cast. Before you begin to use the term "cast" in the comparison of bows, there are a few qualifying factors you need to know. The first of these is an understanding of how much *draw weight* is exerted on the limb when it is drawn to a given arrow length. If the bow is drawn back a distance of twenty-four inches (*draw length*) with a draw weight of forty-five pounds, and the bow is generally capable of the twenty-four inch draw, then this bow is known as a forty-five pound bow. If we put a twenty-two inch arrow to the same bow, the change in the *draw length* will also change the draw weight. Therefore, it is very important to know the draw weight in terms of the draw length.

Given this relationship, shouldn't two bows of the same wood, equal length, and equal weight cast an arrow an equal distance? It is highly unlikely! One of the two bows will draw better and cast farther than the other because of inherent differences in the grain of the wood. Sap

within the wood; the placement of growth rings within the limb; the manner in which the limb was cured, involving temperature and humidity; and even the time of year or month that the limb was cut, will all affect the ability of the limb to store and release energy.

Cast is also affected by the type of wood and/or backing used in the manufacture of the bow. Again, some woods are better for bows than others and some bow designs work better with different woods. For instance, lemon wood and Oregon yew are highly desirable woods

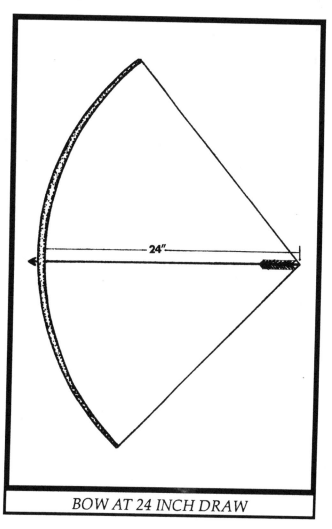

BOW AT 24 INCH DRAW

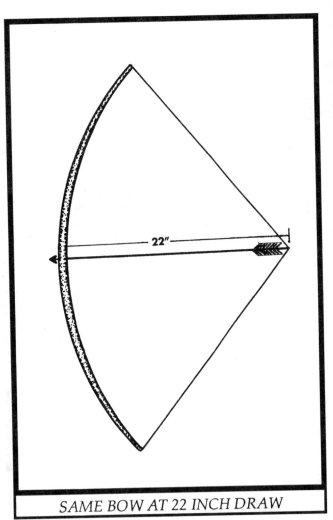

SAME BOW AT 22 INCH DRAW

Koeppen tested the compression values of various woods. The results (*see Page 9*) are interesting because the woods with the highest and lowest compressive factors are not necessarily whose which make the best or the poorest bows, respectively. One of the major keys in making a bow is knowing the point at which the bow *stacks up*, or reaches near-failure compression. The amount of pressure the belly can withstand is a factor we can't change without actually changing the material used for the belly and this will be discussed in depth later in this book. The ability of the bow to withstand tension on the back, however, is something we can easily manipulate. By simply using a *backing material*, we can increase the ability of the bow to withstand more tension. This, of course, can not be done to the *self bow* as, by definition, it has no backing.

for long bows, but they are not useable for short bows. Hickory and ash make great short bows, but are rather slow for the longer bows. Each of these woods are best suited to different bow designs. Hickory and juniper work well for a thin, wide-limbed bow, while birch does not. Osage makes a very fast rectangular bow, but hickory is far less quick in this design.

✠ ✠ ✠

There are two sides to the bow: The *belly*, or part which faces the archer as the bow is drawn, and the *back*, which faces the target as the bow is drawn. Two things occur when a bow is drawn: The back comes under tension and, at the same time, the belly is compressed. The ability of wood to handle this combination of compression/tension varies with the type of wood. T. M. Hamilton (1972:60) and Robert

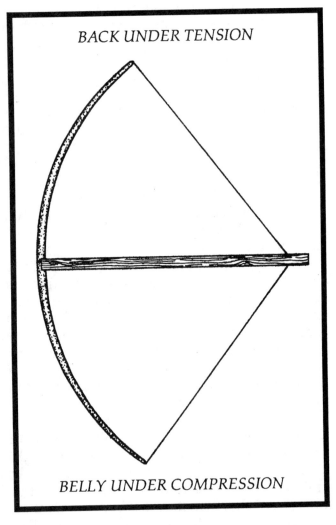

BACK UNDER TENSION

BELLY UNDER COMPRESSION

Pounds Per Square Inch	
Eastern Red Cedar	6,020
White Oak	7,440
Black Locust	10,800
Osage Orange	9,800
Pacific Yew	9,220
Rocky Mountain Juniper	4,200
	(estimate)

HAMILTON/KOEPPEN TEST RESULTS

The self bow was the predominate bow type made and used through the mid-1860s. Many of us made a self bow of some quality when we were kids, and many made a bow of better quality in the school shop. The longbow of the British is a classic example of the self bow.

⌘ ⌘ ⌘

Making an Indian self bow is generally the antithesis of making a European self bow as its construction defies all practical principles of bow making. Because most materials (including wood) withstand tension better than compression, and the back of the bow is under tension while the belly under compression, logic suggests that there should be more wood on the belly than on the back. Further, the back of the self bow should always be flat in order to distribute the tension evenly over its surface.

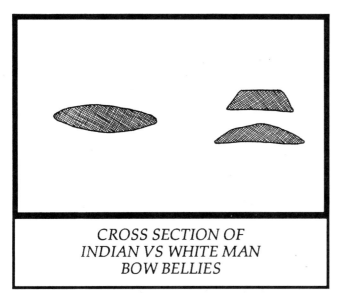

*CROSS SECTION OF
INDIAN VS WHITE MAN
BOW BELLIES*

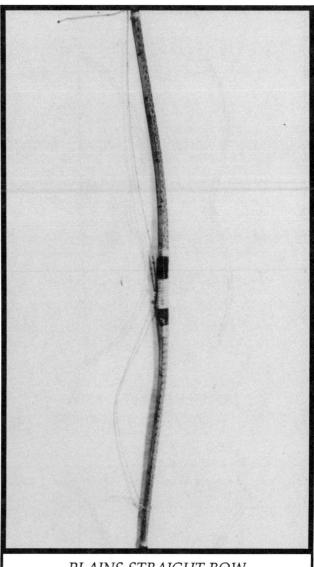

*PLAINS STRAIGHT BOW
(Notice String Follow)*

Shouldn't the belly also be flat in order to distribute the compression evenly? Logically yes, but this is rarely the case with Indian flat style bows. The belly in these bows is usually somewhat convex or rounded in shape. This design works well as long as there is a straight surface near or at the middle of the belly that will take the brunt of the compression load. The wood cells of many bow woods will collapse and lose their ability to withstand this load; this does not mean the bow will break, it simply *follows the string.*

Plains or California self bows are generally of

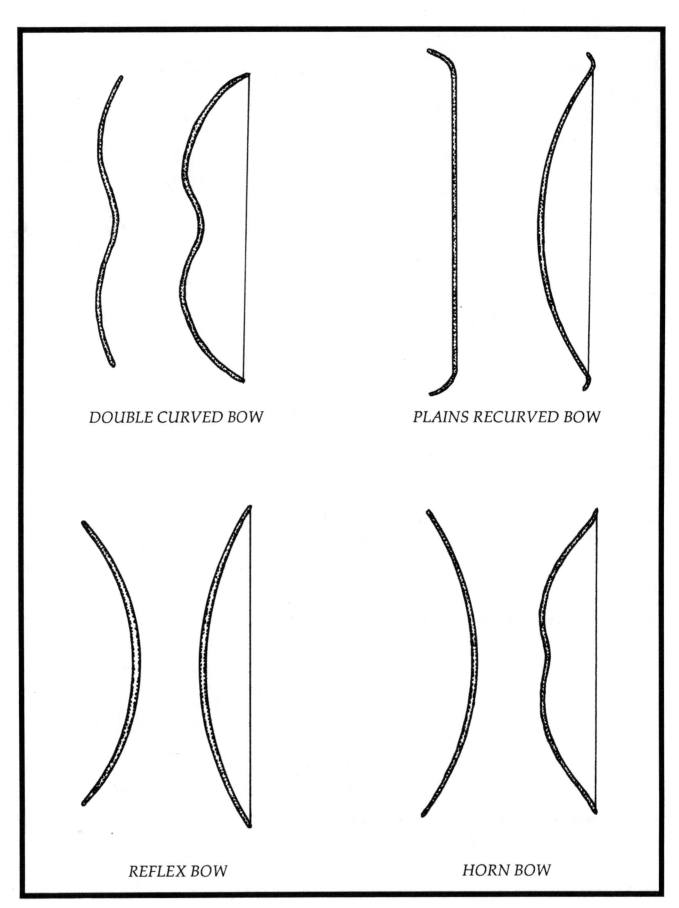

DOUBLE CURVED BOW

PLAINS RECURVED BOW

REFLEX BOW

HORN BOW

The D bow could easily be modified by heat and turned into a reflex self bow, or a double curved bow. The double curved bow is sometimes referred to as a triple curved bow. This design produces a slow bow, although it bucks in the shooting hand and looks nearly the same when braced as it does relaxed. It also resembles Cupid's Bow to some degree. Although quite popular on the Plains, California bowyers never adopted this design; it is a poor shooter.

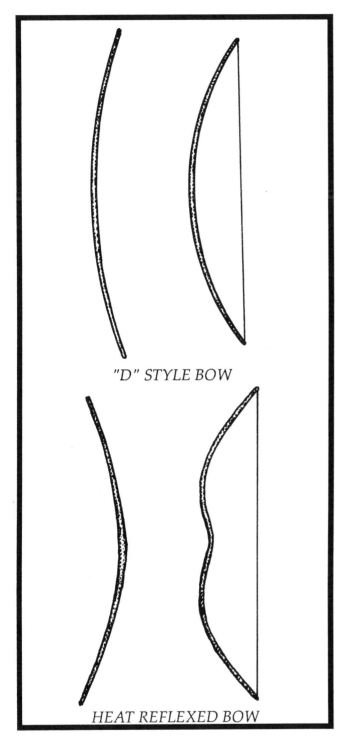

"D" STYLE BOW

HEAT REFLEXED BOW

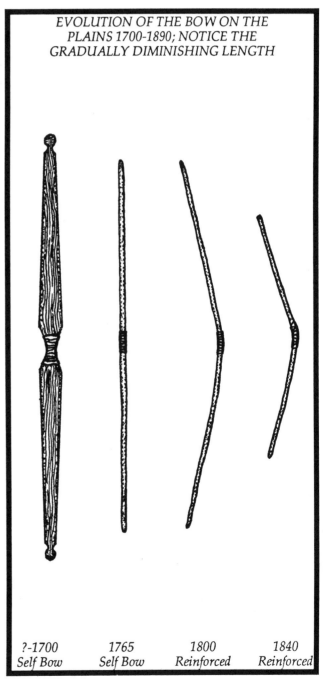

EVOLUTION OF THE BOW ON THE PLAINS 1700-1890; NOTICE THE GRADUALLY DIMINISHING LENGTH

| ?-1700 Self Bow | 1765 Self Bow | 1800 Reinforced | 1840 Reinforced |

three types. These types may have different shapes, but their bow actions are similar. The least common in the Plains or California area is the stick or *D Bow*. The D bow is given its name because it looks like the letter "D" when strung. The D bow was quite often sinew backed, thus making it a *reflex* bow.

The last type of self bow is the reflex or recurve bow (*see Illustrations*). The reflex can be created using either sinew or heat. Most types of wood will draw into a reflex with the use of sinew and the design of the self bow reflex is quite efficient and was very popular. The reflex allows greater energy to be stored in the limb to be released. However, if a bow is reflexed too much, it cannot store all the energy it generates and limb failure will result. Self bows of all these types were prevalent on the North American continent for a long time and remained popular even after the invention of the backed bow.

The self bow quickly evolved into a reinforced or backed bow with the arrival of horses on the Plains (*circa* 1700), as the use of the horse required a short bow with a lot of energy. Before the advent of the horse, most bows were fifty-five to sixty inches in length. Few woods could store the required energy in such short lengths without breaking after limited use. As bows became shorter, the need for backing increased. Sinew was the most widely used backing material although rawhide was also common. Combinations of rawhide/sinew and sinew/canvas have also been observed. Sinew when placed in any abundance on the back of the bow, draws the limbs in a reverse motion so that the limbs not *braced* (strung) will face away from the shooter rather than straight up.

As we discuss the *reflex* bow, keep in mind that the Indian reflex is substantially different from the modern day reflex. The modern reflex is the opposite of the traditional bow, and is quite inefficient when compared to the original design.

Another type of bow is the *horn bow*; this was the last bow developed on this continent and is the most difficult to make. The California Indians never did adapt to the horn bow, and few Indians ever owned one. There are currently fewer than fifty horn bows in museums across the country. As of this writing, I have made bows of elk horn and Texas longhorn. The most desirable horn is that of the bighorn

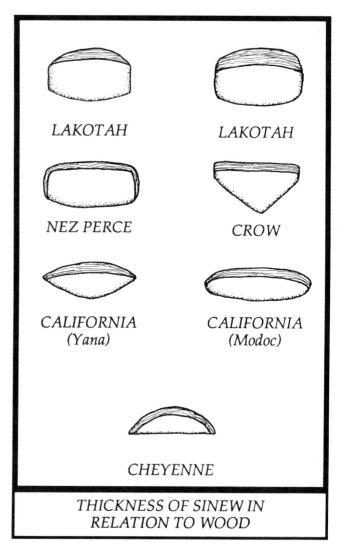

LAKOTAH   LAKOTAH

NEZ PERCE   CROW

CALIFORNIA   CALIFORNIA
(Yana)   (Modoc)

CHEYENNE

*THICKNESS OF SINEW IN
RELATION TO WOOD*

sheep, but it is very difficult to get your hands on at a reasonable price.

✠ ✠ ✠

Listed below are some bow designs you can use. Pay particular attention to the materials used and to the method of manufacture.

PLAINS FLAT BOW. This was the most common type of bow in the Western States and has been found in various lengths from twenty-five inches to fifty inches. It was usually much longer in the Eastern States. The *limbs* can be as wide as two to two and one-half inches just above the handle, with a thickness of three-eighths inches at mid-limb. This is a modified version of the Sudbury bow (below) which was

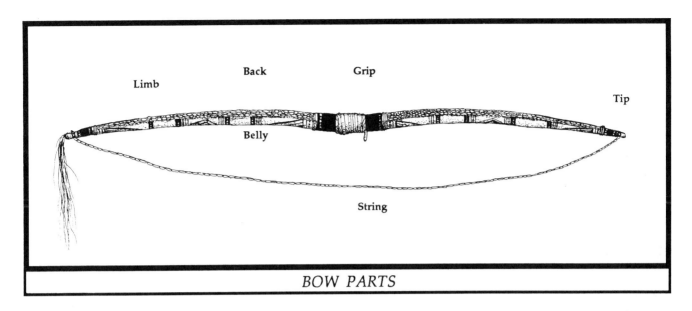

BOW PARTS

found in 1660. Almost any kind of wood will make an excellent flat bow with the exception of yew and lemon wood. Birch is also too brash for this kind of bow. This bow is found in many designs and styles, as it can be backed with sinew, wood or rawhide and be reflexed or recurved with no trouble. Keep in mind that with this bow the back must always be flat while the belly can have any number of shapes. The bellies I have observed have been flat, convex or slightly rounded. The handle is usually quite thin and bends quite a bit in the handle.

CALIFORNIA FLAT BOW. This is almost a total reverse of the Plains flat bow because of the shape of the limbs. Note that with this style, the bow is widest at mid-limb and narrows in both directions. This type of bow was generally recurved and created a reflex of its own because of the sinew backing. They were almost always sinew backed. These bows were usually thirty-eight to fifty inches long, two to four inches wide, and three-sixteenths to one-half inch thick. Pacific yew, juniper, hickory, ash, and black locust all make great California bows. These bows are great shooters.

PLAINS TRIANGULAR BOW. This is a variation of the flat bow, but it is much narrower and a bit thicker. This kind of bow is excellent for high bow weights and is easy to make. The

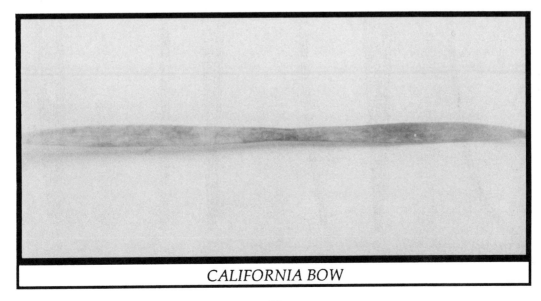

CALIFORNIA BOW

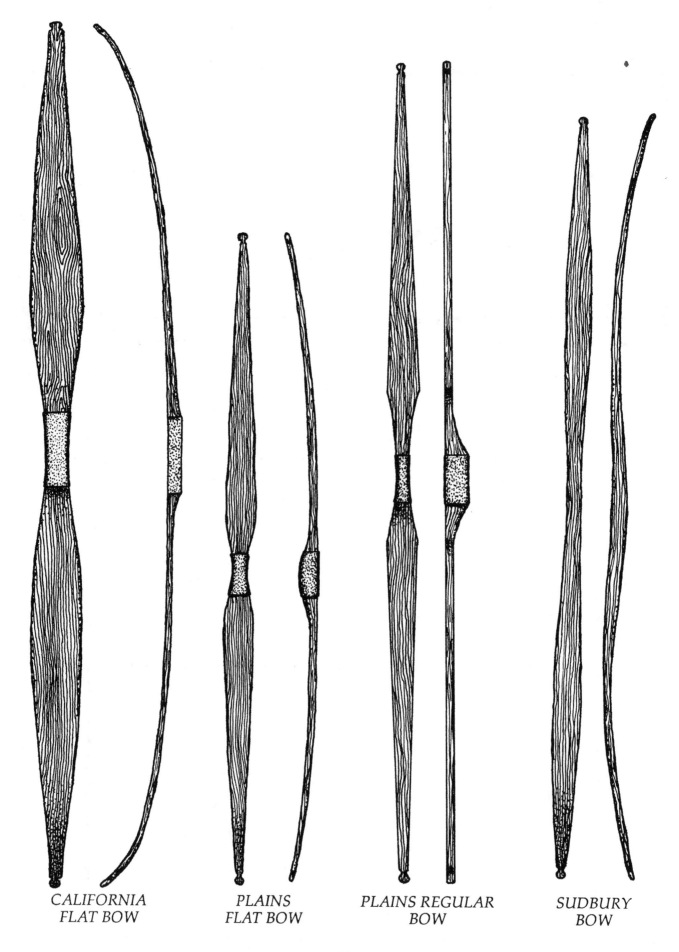

CALIFORNIA
FLAT BOW

PLAINS
FLAT BOW

PLAINS REGULAR
BOW

SUDBURY
BOW

TABULATION OF BOW PERFORMANCES

Tribe, etc.	Material and Type	Length in inches	Dimensions: Grip Mid-limb Below nocks	Draw in inches	Weight in pounds	Cast in yards	Comments/ Reference
Turkish flight bow	Composite	?	?	?	?	482	By Mamhood Effendij in 1795 (Klopsteg, p. 2)
Turkish flight bow	Composite	?	?	?	?	972	Sultan Selim, 1798, (Klopsteg, p. 3)
English target bow	Yew	?	?	28?	48	220	Imported (Pope, 1923 B, p. 44)
English yew flight bow	Yew	?	?	28?	65	300	(Pope, 1923 B, p. 44)
Old English longbow, hunting	Oregon yew	68	1-1/4 x 1-1/8 1-1/8 x 7/8 5/8 x 5/8	28	75	250	Replica by Pope.
Composite flight bow	Composite catgut back	48	? 1-1/4 x 3/4	29	85	274	Replica by Pope. Special 30" flight arrow.
English longbow stave	Oregon yew	76-3/4	4-1/2" circumfrance 4" circumfrance ?	28 36 36	52 72 72	185 212 117	Replica by Pope of "Mary Rose" stave. Shooting English war arrow.
The above stave	Oregon yew	72	? ? ?	28	62	227	Above cut down. Regular flight arrow again used.
The same stave	Oregon yew	68	?	28	70	245	Again cut down. Same flight arrow.
Sudbury bow, Peabody	Red Hickory	67-1/4	1-3/16 x 15/16 9/16 x 1-3/4 3/8 x 3/4	28	46	173	Replica by Pope. Dimensions by Dr. Greengo.
Alaskan	Douglas fir, sinew-corded	56	1-1/2 x 3/4 ? 1 x 5/8	26	80	180	Eskimo Bow
Sioux	?	?	?	?	45	165	(Pope, 1923B, p. 43)
South American	Palma Brava	74	7/8 x 5/8 3/4 x 1/2 1/2 x 3/8	28	50	98	Slow action. Bad design.
Tomawata	?	?	?	?	40	148	(Pope, 1923B, p. 43)
Yurok, reflexed	Yew, sinew-backed	54	1-7/8 x 1/2 2 x 3/8 1 x 3/8	28	30	140	Bends at grip. Flabby cast. Bucks.
Yukon, with bridge	Birch	68	1-1/2 x 1 1-3/8 x 3/4 1 x 1/2	25	60	125	Twists in hand. Poor shooter.
Yaqui	Osage orange	59-1/2	1-1/2 x 7/8 1-1/4 x 5/8 1 x 3/8	28	70	210	Best bow tested.
Yana, slightly recurved	Red yew, rawhide-backed	55	1-5/8 x 5/8 1-3/4 x 1/2 3/4 x 3/8	28	48	205	An Ishi bow. Excellent workmanship.
Paraguay	Ironwood?	71	1-1/4 x 1 1-1/2 x 7/8 9/16 x 3/8	25	60	170	Poor workmanship Excellent wood.
Same bow retillered	Ironwood?	67	?	28	85	265	Regular flight arrow used.
Same bow unchanged	Ironwood?	67	?	28	85	276	Special flight arrow with reduced feathers.
Apache, double-curved	White hickory. Wagon hoop. Sinew-backed	41	1-5/8 x 1-5/8 7/8 x 1/2 5/8 x 3/8	22	28	120	Native arrow 24" long. Flight arrow used.

TABULATION OF BOW PERFORMANCES (Con't.)

Tribe, etc.	Material and Type	Length in inches	Dimensions: Grip Mid-limb Below nocks	Draw in inches	Weight in pounds	Cast in yards	Comments/ Reference
Blackfoot, slight reflex, no backing	Ash?	47-1/2	1-3/8 x 3/4 1-1/4 x 9/16 3/4 x 3/8	25	45	145	Poor shooter. Bucked in hand.
Blackfoot, reflexed	Red Hickory, sinew-backed	40	1-3/8 x 5/8 1-1/4 x 1/2 3/4 x 1/2	20	40	153	Buffalo bow. Sweet shooter
Cheyenne	Ash, sinew-backed	45	1-1/4 x 7/8 1-1/8 x 3/4 7/8 x 5/8	20 24	65 80	156 ?	
Cree	Ash	44	1-5/8 x 1/2 1-3/8 x 7/16 1 x 3/8	20	38	150	Broke at 20" draw.
Hupa, strong reflex	Yew sinew-	47	1-1/2 x 1/2 2-1/4 x 3/8 7/8 x 7/16	22	40	148	Bends in center. Bucks in hand.
Luiseno	Willow	55-1/2	1-1/2 x 3/4 1-1/2 x 5/8 1 x 1/2	26	48	125	Jarring recoil. Poor weapon.
Navajo	Mesquite, sinew-backed	44	1 x 3/4 7/8 x 5/8 1/2 x 1/2	26	45	150	Well-made. Tillered.
Mohave	Willow	67	1-3/8 x 1 1-1/8 x 3/4 3/4 x 1/2	28	40	110	Whip-ended. Flabby cast/
Osage	Osage orange	47-1/2	7/8 x 7/8 1-1/2 x 1/2 5/8 x 3/8	20	40	92	Poor bow for wood used.

The Table of Bow Performances that is printed above was derived from tests done by Dr. Saxton Pope from 1918 to 1924. Dr. Pope has been called the "father" of Native American archery studies and his writings are still among the most current and concise publications available today.

In order to perform these tests and comparisons, one would have needed the respect and trust of many museums. Dr. Pope had such trust. He was able to draw upon these bow collections of note: University of California, the Jessop Collection, and the American Museum of Natural History. The tests, as he performed them, were fair, informative and thorough.

As Dr. Pope noted (1923:33), "... the attempt in every test was to get out of the bow all the cast that was in it. No implement was spared out of respect for its age or apparent infirmity. . . The elevation at which each arrow was projected was approximately forty-five degrees from the horizontal, a quick release was given upon full draw. . ."

These tables are reproduced through the courtesy of T. M. Hamilton and the University of California Press.

handles seem to sweep into the limbs making the bow bend the most in the middle of the limbs. These bows come in every length from thirty-five to fifty-five inches and are three-quarters of an inch wide just above the handle. The bow at mid-limb would be about five-sixteenths of an inch thick. If this bow was changed at all, it was nearly always recurved.

PLAINS RECTANGULAR BOW. The rectan-gular bow was a popular style until the advent of the horse made it less popular because it is a difficult bow to make in short lengths. The rectangular bow was usually a double curved or a heat induced reflex bow. This bow seems to have made a comeback between the late 1800s and early 1900s. This may have been due to a lack of the horses, the availability of milled woods, or a desire to return to a more tradi-tional lifestyle. These bows are usually in

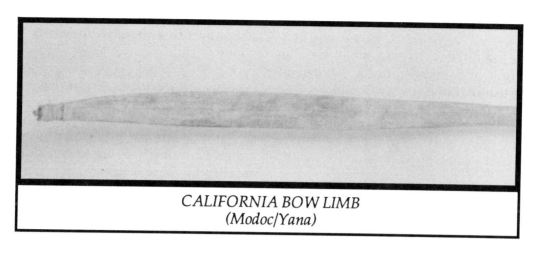

CALIFORNIA BOW LIMB
(Modoc/Yana)

lengths of forty-eight inches or longer. The center, or handle of the bow, measures about one inch square, the mid-limb measures seven-eighths by five-eighths of an inch, and the tips measure one-half by three-eighths of an inch.

THE SUDBURY BOW. This is the oldest known North American Indian bow. This bow was collected at the home of William Goodnough in Sudbury, Massachusetts in the year 1660. It seems an Indian was shot while trying to run from the home and the bow was kept as a "souvenir" of the occasion. The bow is made of red hickory and has a tip to tip measurement of sixty-seven and one-eighth inches. The nock to nock measurement is sixty-five inches, the grip is one and three-sixteenths by fifteen-sixteenths inches, with a mid-limb measurement of nine-sixteenths by one and seven eighths inches.

Due to the age of the bow, it has never been strung nor shot by anyone interested in the physical aspects of the bow. Dr. Saxton Pope made a replica of this bow from the measurements of the original. The replica drew a weight of forty-six pounds at twenty-eight inches, and had a cast of one hundred, seventy-three yards. Remember, no two bows perform alike due to differences in wood, so while the replica gives us some idea of what the bow was like it may have actually been a better or worse bow.

⌗ ⌗ ⌗

The information concerning the Sudbury bow is given to provide a direct comparison to the bows of the Plains and California tribes. The Sudbury appears to be a finely made bow with a great deal of thought given to its design. This type of bow does not appear in any other collection, so progress seems to have quickly replaced this style with a faster or more effi-

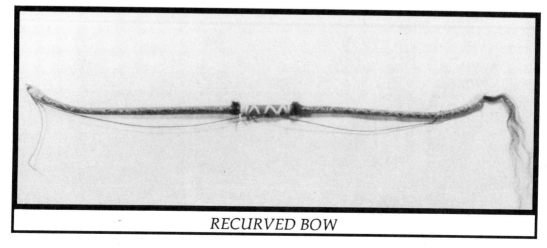

RECURVED BOW

17

cient kind.

None of the Plains bows in existence today has a draw weight over sixty pounds. To have a short bow with that much draw weight would be an incredible feat of manufacture, let alone the task of drawing it back on a running horse and shooting it with any accuracy. Keep this in mind as you are selecting a bow style, weight and length.

Use the illustrations in this book or in other Indian archery related publications to help you come to a decision. Most museums are happy to allow you to examine a part of their collection if you take the time to explain what you are doing. If you feel uncomfortable using a specific bow design, then use this book as a guide or reference, not as a manual written in stone. Use some imagination, I'm sure that Indian bowyers did.

It is important to remember that anyone can make a bow, but it takes a good bowyer to extract the best potential from the stave and turn it into a living, breathing thing of art. The manner in which the bow is *tillered* (the art of making the bow bend equally in both limbs) is of utmost importance, much more so than the finish or design of the bow. Most Plains bows were poorly tillered, but every tribe had a good bowyer, and every man had an extra stave or two seasoned in his lodge. This is a luxury most of us cannot afford, so make your bow with the utmost care and craftsmanship.

CUTTING THE WOOD

Once you are comfortable with the type or style of bow you want, its time to make the first cut. If the stave is not the length you desire or if it has a twist in one end, this is the time to cut it to size. One way the Indians used to measure bow length was to stand straight with an arm perpendicular to the ground. Holding the palm out flat, they measured the distance from their palm to the ground. This would be the height of the bow and it was usually about waist high. The tip measurement was derived from the thickness of the little finger, and the grip thickness determined by closing the thumb over the end of the index finger, forming an *O*. The space inside the "O" would be the thickness of the grip.

I have never used these units of measurements, nor have I met any other bowyer who does. There are, however, several historians that stand by this claim for bow dimensions, so there must be some merit to it. Using this scale, most of the bows I have examined would have belonged to very short Indians. More likely, they were made to a convenient size for use on horse back. So, determine the bow length that will personally satisfy you.

When you have done this, find the exact middle of the stave and mark it. Add three inches from the center line in both directions. This will be the handle of the bow. Now look at the stave.

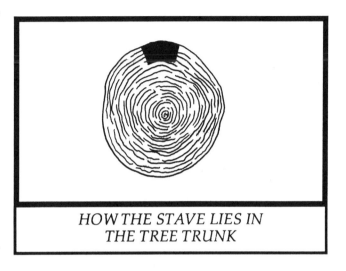

HOW THE STAVE LIES IN THE TREE TRUNK

The part of the wood that is nearest the bark is called the *sapwood*. This will become the back of the bow and faces away from you as you shoot. The part that you see as you shoot is called the *belly* and consists of the wood from nearest the center of the log. As you work the wood down to create the bow, <u>all of your major cutting, filing and scraping will be done on the belly</u>.

At the end of each limb, mark the exact center. Add a quarter inch on either side of this mark for the width of the tip. Now draw a line from the outside edge of the handle to the line marking the outside edge of the tip. Do this on each side of each limb. If you are making a Califor-

STAVE MARKED AND READY FOR SHAPING

nia bow, a french curve is very helpful at this point. Be sure that the curves drawn on the California bow are even on each side or there will be problems as you proceed.

Starting at the outer lines on your handle, begin tapering the wood to a thinner point near the tips until you have cut to the lines previously marked. The bow is now cut to length and width. Next mark a line on the belly three inches from each tip and begin tapering the belly to this line. From the line to the tip, taper the ends of the bow back up to a slightly larger size. This adds mass to the ends and will improve the cast of the bow; this also helps to prevent *crystalizing* in the event that you wish to recurve the limbs. A few of the old bows I have examined have the heavier tips, so while not common, it is authentic. It also improves the performance of the bow.

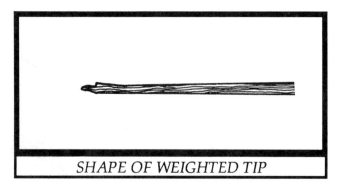

SHAPE OF WEIGHTED TIP

As you taper from the middle to the tips, take wood off the sides in equal amounts. The middle of the old time flat bows was usually twice the width of the tips. If this is a Modoc/Yana bow, the opposite is usually true.

✠ ✠ ✠

One major difference between the handles of most Plains bows and those of "white man" bows is that the Plains bows lack what is called the *Buchanan's Dip*. White man bows are generally longer than the Indian bows and have a stiff, stationary handle. Therefore, white man bows bend only one third of the bow on each limb and only two-thirds of the bow actually functions. Plains bows are short and the entire bow must be active. This can create a bit of *kick* in the bow handle, especially in the California

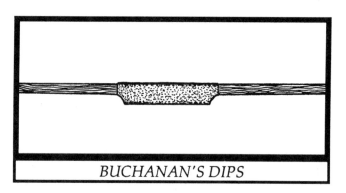

BUCHANAN'S DIPS

types. Incidentally, a bow with Buchanan's Dip cannot be reflexed without twisting the limbs. Recurved, yes; reflexed, no.

✠ ✠ ✠

After you have worked with the stave for awhile and it has begun to resemble a bow, if you feel confident that you have cut a fairly consistent amount of wood from each limb, remove any bark that is on the back. Do this by scraping it off rather than using a draw knife or a plane. Once the bark is removed you can check the bow's progress.

Place one end of the bow on the ground with the back facing you. Put one hand on the handle and the other hand on the limb that is in the air. Hold the tip firmly so that it doesn't move and pull the handle toward you. Look closely at how the limbs bend. Do this in a quiet room so that you can relax the bow if there is any cracking sound. This process is called *rough tillering* the bow. If you do hear a crack, don't panic. Even if the wood has cracked a bit the stave can usually be saved with some patience and care.

If you were watching the limbs closely, you should have seen whether or not the bow was bending evenly on both limbs. If you could not see what the limbs were doing, there is another way to check for the tiller of the bow: Stand in front of a mirror and place the handle of the bow on your head, belly down. Grasp each tip and slowly pull them downward. Watch the limbs in the mirror very carefully. You will hear any cracking sound sooner this way as the sound will be amplified through your skull.

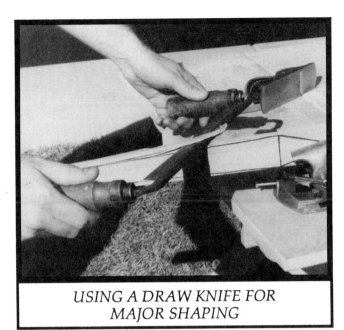

USING A DRAW KNIFE FOR
MAJOR SHAPING

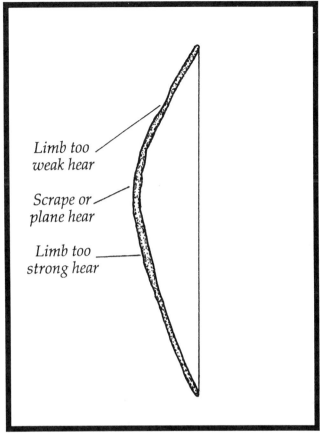

Limb too
weak hear

Scrape or
plane hear

Limb too
strong hear

Quickly release the wood if any cracking noise is heard.

If the bow is not bending uniformly as you pull the limbs down, or if it feels stronger on one limb, mark where it is stronger or bending unevenly. Scrape or plane the stiffest limb. Most beginning bowyers do not remove enough wood at the handle, so watch this point carefully. Remember, the bow should arc or curve in balance throughout the limbs.

As you remove more wood from the stiff limb, check your progress from time to time. A *tillering board* or jig is helpful at this point. This tool will allow you to step back for a moment and see what you are accomplishing.

✠ ✠ ✠

To make a tillering board, get a thirty inch two by four. Cut a saddle or notch at one end big enough to hold the bow handle. This notch should be padded so that the handle does not slip out. Do not make the notch too big or the bow will move from side to side. Measure six inches down from the saddle and place a nail, dowel, or notch every two inches from the end. This is to hold the tillering string. To make a tillering string, all you need is a bit of clothes-line rope or thin cord at least twelve inches

longer than the bow. Loop each end. You will also need to cut a notch or nock in each tip using one of two methods:

First, you may cut one nock at the very end on the edge of the tip. The bow cannot be shot with this kind of nock, but it works well for tillering the bow. Try not to cut into the back. A nice consequence of using the temporary single nock is that you are free to decide what your final nock design will be at a later time. It helps to use duct or electrical tape to hold the tillering string in place; this is a safety precaution, but I once had a tillering string let go while using the tillering board. The bow flew wild and broke, wasting all the time I had spent curing the wood, shaping the bow, and being proud of what appeared to be a fine weapon.

The second method is to decide the type of final nock you wish to have and roughly cut them into the wood at this stage. Again, be careful of cutting into the back, especially with this method. Once the nock is cut, there is no

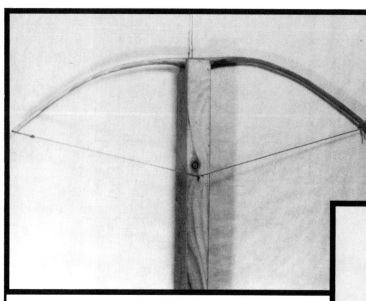

IMPERFECT ARC THAT
NEEDS WORK

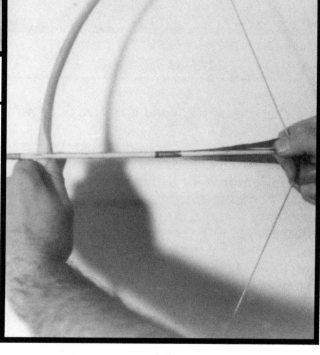

BOW ON LEFT SHOWN BELOW
WITH PERFECT TILLER

turning back unless you shorten the overall length of the bow. Many of the Plains bows with cut-in nocks have two nocks at the top, and one nock on the bottom. Some have only one nock to place the string on with the other end of the string tied to the end of the bow. A few bows have even been drilled so that the string can be permanently tied. Many bows, particularly bows with sinew backs, have nocks of built-up sinew. This is especially true

of bows from the far Northern Plains.

Put the tillering string on the bow, tape the nocks if you need to, and place the bow in the tillering jig or board. Pull the string to the first notch and hook it there, then step back and observe what the limbs are doing. Note where the limbs differ from one another in the way that they bend. Once again, scrape or plane the stiffest limb. If the limbs are fairly similar in the way they bend, plane them only one or two times between checks on the tillering jig. If you take too much wood from the stiffer limb, you must balance the once-weaker limb to the limb you have been working on. You can always take wood off, but you can never put it back on.

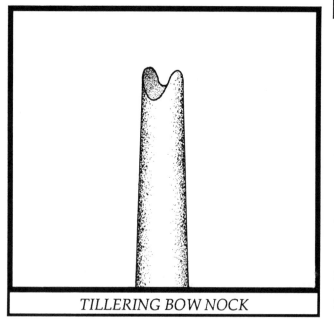

TILLERING BOW NOCK

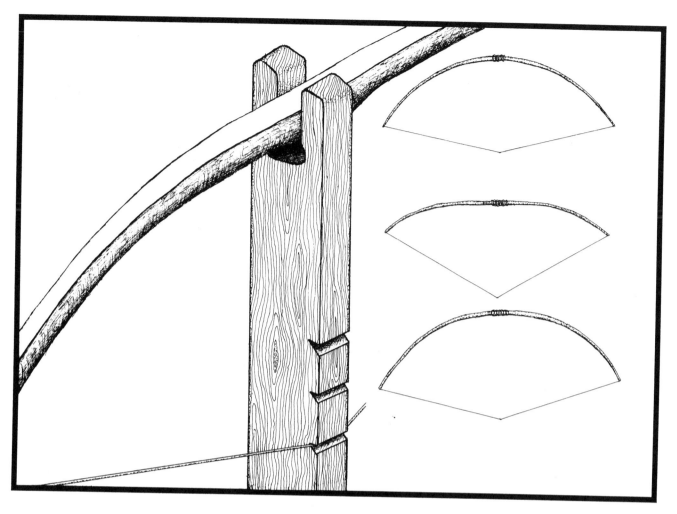

If you get carried away, your forty-five pound masterpiece can end up as a fifteen pound child's toy. Be very careful at this stage.

After the bow is tillered properly, hold it in your hand as though you were going to shoot it. Pull on the tillering string as though there were an arrow to the bow. Be sure to draw it only three-quarters of the way back or until it feels as though it is *stacking* or under too much

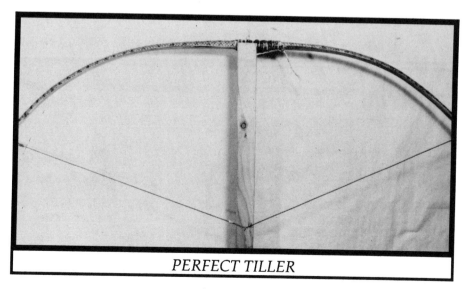

PERFECT TILLER

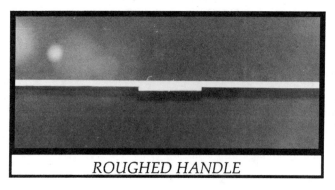

ROUGHED HANDLE

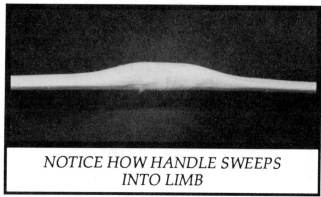

NOTICE HOW HANDLE SWEEPS INTO LIMB

compression. Is the draw weight right for you? If the draw weight is too low, you can fix this later as explained in the chapter on backings. If the draw weight is too high, you need to scrape or plane both limbs in equal amounts. If this is necessary, take two passes with the plane on one limb, then take two passes on the other limb. Scraping one-on-one, limb for limb, results in very little re-tillering of the bow when the weight is correct.

Mid-Plains and California bows drop weight very quickly if a pass is made along the belly from handle to tip with a sharp plane. Northern Plains bows retain tiller and drop weight quickly if you work on the sides as opposed to the belly. No matter how you trim the weight, do it evenly over the entire limb to save energy, time and mistakes when re-tillering.

Although a bow scale is helpful at this point, it certainly is not a necessity. Knowing the exact draw weight or targeting the bow to a specific weight is nearly impossible, so it is difficult to pre-plan a forty-five pound bow; you may end

up with a forty-three pound bow or a forty-seven pound bow. Even if you follow the charts for bow sizes in this book exactly, you will still get results that are different from the chart weight measurements. If your bow is a bit lighter than you wish, we can fix that problem later. If the weight is still a bit heavier than you want, do not scrape or plane anymore until you finish the next step. The *handle, center grasp* or *riser* (all three terms are correct), is the next link in the chain.

At this point your handle is fairly wide and uncomfortable to hold. The ends of the handle should blend smoothly into the limbs, so you may only need to balance out the width and thickness at the grip. White man bows have an arrow rest cut into the handle, but we are making Indian bows and the arrow rests upon the hand. We want comfort but that does not mean we need an arrow rest or a grip that is cut to each finger. There is no predetermined amount of wood to cut away for a proper grip. Use the rasp, shoemakers file or a round chunk

NOCK STYLES

| *Modoc/Yana* | *Common to Many Plains Tribes* | *Cheyenne* | *Eastern Plains* | *Nez Perce or Arapaho* |

24

of sandstone to file the grip into a flat oval. Once again, cut into the back as little as possible, although you must file into it a bit. Make the grip fit your hand. File the side down enough for the arrow to stay in place easily once your hand is under it. Don't file down to the point where the arrow is flushed. On modern bows the string is centered exactly with the arrow rest so that the arrow leaves the bow directly in the string's path. This is why modern bows are fired in the Mediterranean fashion: Arms extended, bow perfectly vertical and hand-anchored to the chin. Indian archery is quite different and if you try to place the string directly flush with the open portion of

the grip, your handle will be too thin, the bow will reflex too much, and it will probably break as explained in the chapter on Shooting.

⌘ ⌘ ⌘

At this point, the bow is fairly well seasoned, nearly tillered, and the grip is cut to fit; all that is left to do is to cut the final nocks. You may choose to go real old-time and do the nocks entirely out of sinew. You may prefer sinew mixed with cut nocks or wood only nocks. All are fine. On a flat bow, that is not recurved, the sinew nock does not work well unless you make a small knob of sinew directly above the

NOCK STYLES

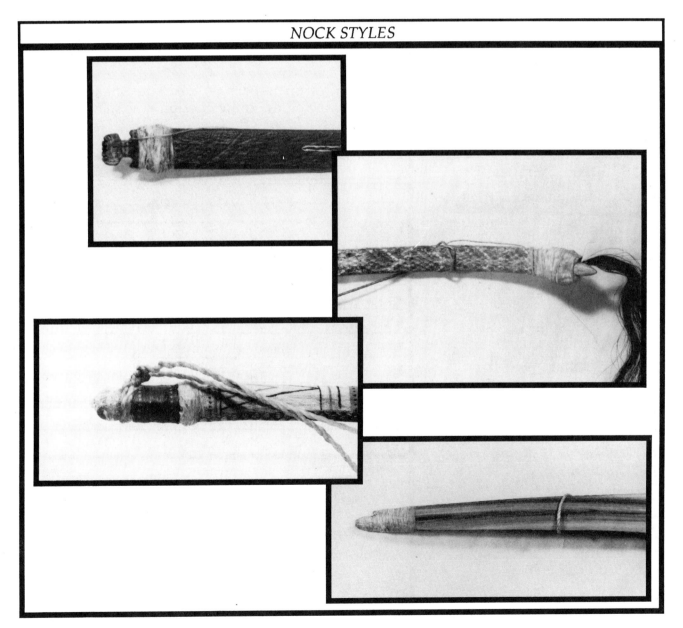

string to hold it on at full draw. Although I have seen only one example of an attached tip on an old-time bow, some bowyers attach carved nocks of elk, cow or buffalo horn. A few have even used nocks carved of different types of wood. Even though this makes your bow a trifle less traditional, it can enhance the appearance and even the speed of your bow as a result of the additional weight.

In any event, choose a nock style that is pleasing to you. Use one of the designs in this book, or create your own. While cutting the nock, with a saw, file or hot nail, be sure to do most of the cutting on the belly and not the back. This rule is doubly important if the bow is to be backed or recurved.

Once the nocks are cut and the grips filed to your satisfaction, check the tiller once again. It is common for it to have changed a bit during the filing of the grip. Smooth out any uneven bends that may have developed, making sure

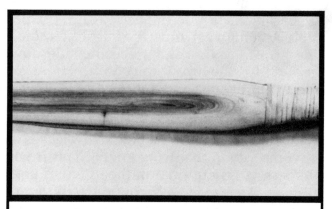

BOW BY C. RINDLISBACHER
Note the Perfect Work Around the Growth Rings

that the bow bends in a perfect arc, and is uniform across each limb. Once this is done and you are satisfied with the curve, pat yourself on the back. You have just created a bow of the oldest known design - the self bow.

25 Lb. - 5'0" Flat Bow

	#	@
At the middle of the bow . . .	14/16"	1 4/16"
4" above the middle (At widening of Limb)	1 5/16"	8/16"
8" above middle	1 5/16"	5/16"
12" above middle	1 5/16"	4/16"
16" above middle	1 4/16"	4/16"
20" above middle	1 1/16"	4/16"
24" above middle	14/16"	4/16"
28" above middle	11/16"	3/16"
Just under the nocks	9/16"	3/16"
At the extreme tip	5/16"	2/16"

40 Lb. Flat Bow

	#	@
At the middle of the bow . . .	15/16"	1 1/4"
4" above the middle (At widening of Limb)	1 3/8"	1/2"
8" above middle	1 3/8"	1/2"
12" above middle	1 3/8"	1/2"
16" above middle	1 1/4"	7/16"
20" above middle	1 3/16"	1/3-1/2"
24" above middle	1"	1/3-1/2"
28" above middle	7/8"	3/8"
32" above middle	3/4"	5/16"
At the nocks (cut in wood)	5/8"	1/4"
At the tip	1/2"	1/4"

Bow is 5'6" Long - 40 lbs. at 26" draw

LEGEND
 # = Width
 @ = Thickness, Back to Belly

LEMONWOOD BOWS - 5'0" LONG

	20 Lbs.		23 Lbs.		25 Lbs.		30 Lbs.		50 Lbs.	
	Across Back	Back to Belly	Across Back	Back to Belly	Across Back	Back to Belly	Across Back	Back to Belly	Across Back	Back to Belly
At the Handle . . .	13/16"	9/16"	13/16"	11/16"	14/16"	12/16"	14/16"	12/16"	14/16"	13/16"
4" Above Handle	12/16"	8/16"	12/16"	10/16"	13/16"	10/16"	13/16"	11/16"	13/16"	12/16"
8" Above Handle	12/16"	7/16"	11/16"	9/16"	12/16"	9/16"	12/16"	10/16"	12/16"	10/16"
12" "	11/16"	6/16"	11/16"	8/16"	12/16"	8/16"	12/16"	9/16"	12/16"	10/16"
16" "	10/16"	6/16"	10/16"	7/16"	11/16"	8/16"	11/16"	8/16"	11/16"	8/16"
20" "	9/16"	6/16"	10/16"	7/16"	10/16"	7/16"	11/16"	7/16"	10/16"	7/16"
24" "	8/16"	5/16"	9/16"	6/16"	9/16"	7/16"	9/16"	7/16"	9/16"	7/16"
At the Nocks . . .	6/16"	5/16"	8/16"	6/16"	7/16"	6/16"	7/16"	6/16"	8/16"	6/16"

These bow charts are for longer bows, but if calipers are used they can be scaled down.
Charts are used courtesy of Wood's Unusual from Stemmler's Archery Workshop,
Pgs. 44 and 54

REFLEX AND RECURVES

Recurving (forming a bow whose tips have been forced back in a direction away from the archer) or *reflexing* (forming a bow that has a definite curve away from the archer when not strung) alters the bow's natural form in order to increase speed or cast. Recurve bows have been used throughout the history of archery and remain popular today. Many of the newer compound bows have adopted some of the principles of the recurved limb.

Reflex bows have also been around for a long time, but are primarily associated with certain cultures. The early Europeans and African tribesmen, for example, never really developed the reflexed limb. As a matter of fact, it was mostly Plains Indians, Turks and Orientals that developed and used a reflex design for their bows. Please note that reflex bows in the primitive sense are not the same as the modern day "reflex" design. Modern bow designs use a reflex that is quite different from the primitive patterns, and is mostly done for aesthetic reasons. The modern reflex is actually less efficient than either a modern flat bow or recurve bow. They also seem to be always *following the string*, resulting in poor limb life.

Many of the Woodland bows were recurved, a design later copied by northeastern Plains bowyers. Few of the Western or Northwestern bows had true recurves, although many had slightly recurved tips. One can easily believe that the Plains peoples knew a fair amount about arrow velocity, balance and draw ratios, based upon similarities of bow design, despite drastic differences in the woods available to them.

Some bow woods accept an unnatural bend more readily than others. Apitong and elm both have difficulties responding to much of a curve, while hickory, ash and locust all bend

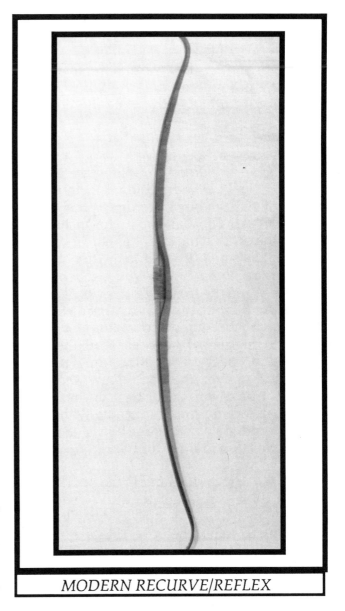

MODERN RECURVE/REFLEX

quite easily. Some woods *sweat* moisture out rather than in, so they become very brittle once curved and dried. Others react to the techniques used to create drastic curves by crystalizing and break very quickly. Throw all your ideas and knowledge about modern day recurves out the window as you will only hurt yourself if you expect a short bow to recurve as

27

much as a longer, more modern bow. The Indian bow does not follow the string as much as a modern recurve and will, therefore, have more snap with one inch of recurve than a modern bow has with six inches of curve.

✠ ✠ ✠

Properly recurving or reflexing a bow is relatively simple, but let me warn you that one mistake left uncorrected can destroy all your hard work. Also, be aware that recurving or reflexing a bow may damage your beautiful tillering job, although this is easily repaired.

Some bowyers have said that to recurve or reflex you must boil the wood. You can do this but placing the wood in boiling water effectively cooks it. The traditional method to recurve or reflex a bow is to dig a pit six inches longer than the bow and about ten inches deep. Tamp the earth in the trench as hard as possible and build a small fire next to the trench. A big fire is not necessary as you need only the embers. Line the trench with rocks or pebbles and cover these with a thin layer of dirt. Fill the trench with water and allow the water to drain down to the level of the rocks. Place the bow in the trench, cover it with dirt, tamp lightly and pour water over the dirt. Now shovel the embers from the fire over the trench from end to end. Keep the embers burning with as little wood as possible and let the bow steam in this setting for two to three hours.

While the bow is steaming in the pit, find a log with a three inch diameter and two one and one-half inch diameter logs. These will be used as forms to reflex the bow. Place a stake on either side of the three inch log so it will not roll.

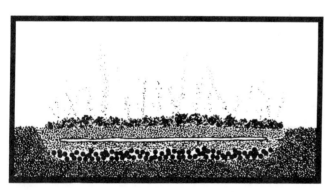

NAILS IN LOG FOR RECURVING

You will not need the smaller logs if you want a single reflex bow. If you are going to recurve the bow, get one log that is about twelve inches around. Drive two nails into the round side at opposite angles so that the heads meet and form an upside down V. This will hold the tip you are recurving.

Remove the embers from the pit and take the bow out of the ground as quickly as possible. To reflex the bow, place the center of the handle, with the back down, over the three inch log. Place the two smaller logs under each of the tips and stand or kneel on the belly in the middle of each limb so that the back is touching the ground between the logs. Rub wet buckskin or a cool wash cloth over the entire bow for about ten minutes, or until the wood is cool. Keep kneeling or standing on the limbs until you are sure that the wood has cooled thoroughly. Once this is accomplished, the reflex is complete.

To recurve the bow the traditional way is more difficult. You will need to work very fast and

*REFLEXING THE BOW BY
USING HEAT AND WEIGHT*

will need a helper for this technique. Wet the log with the nails in it before taking the bow out of the ground. Remove the bow from the trench and insert one of the tips under the nails to just below the nock. Bend the bow to the desired amount of recurve and rub the bend with a cool cloth or a bit of wet hide. Do this quickly. Once the bend has cooled, repeat this process with the other limb. Be sure that the other limb is still hot; if it is allowed to cool you will have to start again with the bow under the ground, etc.

✠ ✠ ✠

If all of this sounds too hard or risky, there is another method: Get a couple of modern style Dutch ovens and some foil. Fill the ovens with water and put them on two adjoining burners on the stove. Once the water is boiling, place the bow over the ovens, with the back down, and cover the two ovens and the bow with foil, arranging it so that the entire bow is receiving steam. Allow the bow to steam for about half an hour to forty minutes. Remove the bow from the steam and reflex it as described above; you can do this on the kitchen floor.

✠ ✠ ✠

The process is nearly the same to recurve, but use only one Dutch oven and do one tip at a time. Let the wood steam for about an hour. Bend the tips as described above, but work less

quickly to avoid mistakes. Be sure to bend each limb to the same curve or the tiller will be incorrect. If you plan to do a lot of bows, you may build a jig with clamps to form each curve equally.

The majority of old bows, particularly those under forty-five inches in length were reflexed. The reflex does not add to the draw weight of the bow, but does add to the speed and, consequently the knock-down power, of an arrow. It is rather odd that a modern compound bow, with a forty-five pound draw weight has an average arrow speed of 200 feet per second (*fps*), while a primitive reflex with sinew on the back and the same draw weight can approach 190 fps. You would expect to gain more than ten feet per second in one thousand years of technological advancement. My point is that primitive reflex bows are efficient even by modern standards, and it is surprising to me that contemporary bow manufacturers do not take advantage of this design. True, a primitive reflex bow has more kick in the handle than a modern bow, and some may argue this affects its accuracy, but primitive archers have learned to compensate for this problem.

✠ ✠ ✠

In either reflex or recurve, do not draw or string the bow for at least a week. Be sure that all the moisture is gone before you move on, letting the wood dry of its own accord. <u>Do Not</u> use a heater or hair dryer to speed the process. It is also a good idea to grease the bow with fat or lard at this time. Do not grease the back if you plan on backing the bow.

When you are confident the bow has dried completely, string it with the tillering string and check the tillering. You may need to fine-tiller the bow again. If the tiller is close and the bow is to be sinew backed, do not tiller at this time. Simply mark the problem and use extra sinew to strengthen a weakness or apply less sinew to correct a strong limb. You may still have to work the belly after sinewing the back.

If the recurve doesn't go as planned, you can always re-heat the bow and try again. On the other hand, it is almost impossible to fix a problem reflex bow because of the number and nature of the curves. Try to look at the bright side as you have gained valuable experience. Good luck.

*BEND THE HOT LIMB UNTIL
IT HAS COOLED*

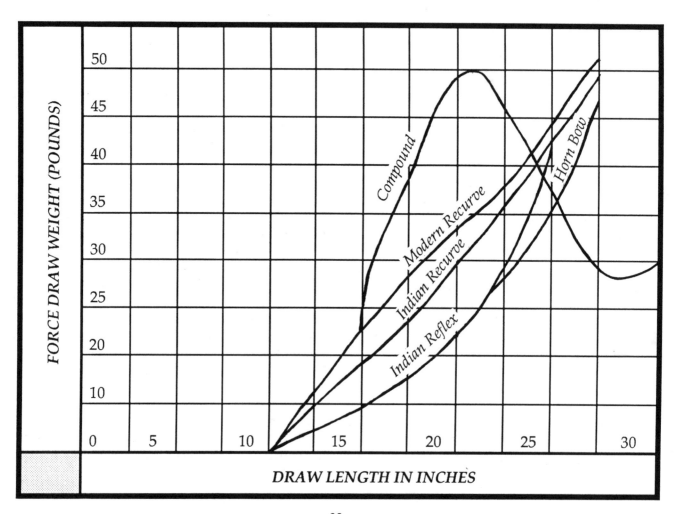

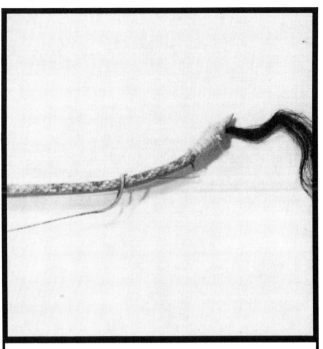

SHARP RECURVE
(Uncommon in Plains Indian Bows)

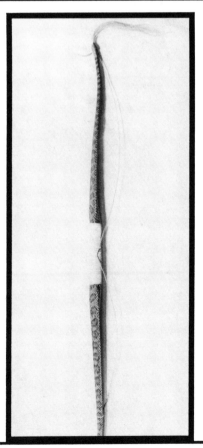

SLIGHT RECURVE
(Fairly Common)

MODERN 50 Lb COMPOUND BOW
ARROW: 400 grains
VELOCITY: 208 FPS

✠ ✠ ✠

MODERN 50 Lb RECURVE BOW
ARROW: 400 grains
VELOCITY: 182 FPS

✠ ✠ ✠

INDIAN 50 Lb RECURVE BOW
(46 inches in length*)
ARROW: 395 grains
VELOCITY: 171 FPS

✠ ✠ ✠

INDIAN 50 Lb REFLEX BOW
(44 inches in length*)
ARROW: 395 grains
VELOCITY: 193 FPS

✠ ✠ ✠

TRADITIONAL 50 Lb LONGBOW
ARROW: 400 grains
VELOCITY: 162 FPS

✠ ✠ ✠

INDIAN 50 Lb HORN BOW
MOUNTAIN SHEEP HORN
(38 inches, tip to tip length*)
ARROW: 375 grains
VELOCITY: 202 FPS

The length of the Indian bows is noted due to the length of the arrow it shoots. Arrow length is shorter in relationship to bow length. This, of course, would alter the testing of various arrow speeds.

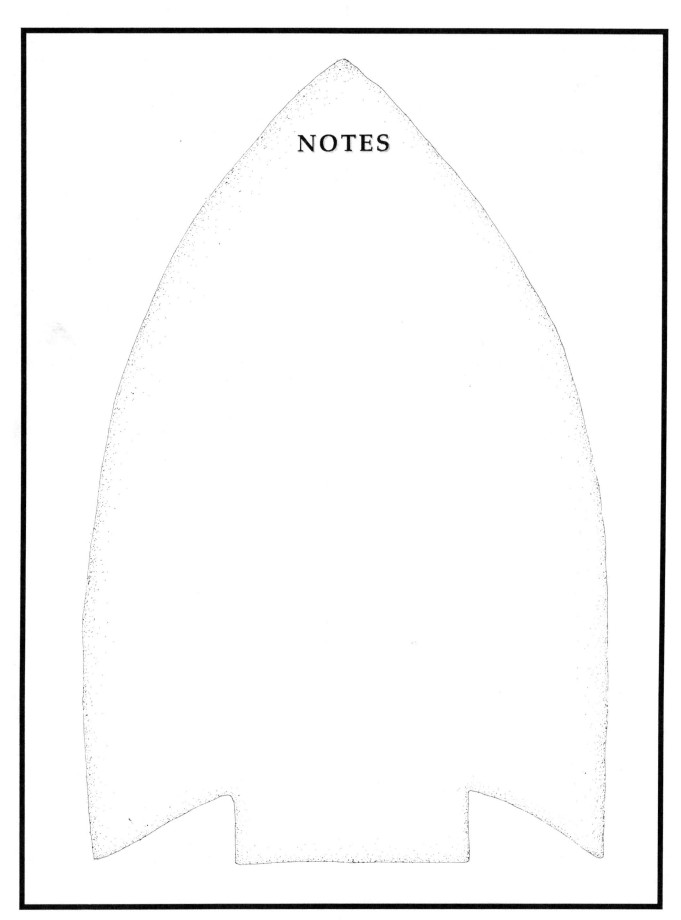

NOTES

BACKING THE BOW

The process of *backing a bow* means placing any substance on the back of the bow with the intention of extending the life of the bow and/or improving the manner in which the bow shoots. Sinew, rawhide, intestine and wood are all materials used for backing a bow. Most California bows which have been researched for this and other publications have either a sinew or a sinew and intestine backing. Fewer than half the Plains bows examined were backed at all but then again, if a man broke a bow he usually had two or three staves seasoned in his lodge. This is a luxury that most of us cannot afford, therefore, backing the bow simply to add longevity is a good idea. A wise old bowyer once told me that a fully drawn bow is seven-eighths broken and backing the bow could stave away that extra eighth.

A *wood backing* means the addition of a thin strip of wood, usually about a quarter inch thick, to the back of the bow. Elm, white hickory, or black locust are all very good woods for backing a bow and a wooden backing will increase the draw strength and cast of a bow if it is properly applied.

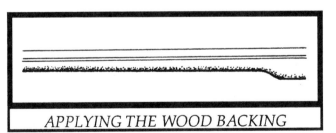

APPLYING THE WOOD BACKING

Make sure that the wood chosen for backing is absolutely free of knots or twists in the grain. Be sure that the back of your bow stave has a flat surface and that the backing material is also flat. Using a saw blade or a rough file, raise the nap of the wood on the back of the bow. Do not cut it, just abrade it from tip to tip so that the

glue will have a good surface to adhere to. Do the same thing to the side of the backing strip that will be glued to the back of the bow. Keep the bow in a warm place, such as in the sun or near a heat vent or stove. Sponge or paint the back of the bow with hide glue or waterproof casein glue. Be liberal with the gluing process as any areas not properly glued will likely cause the premature death of the bow.

Use a dowel that is one-half to three-fourths as wide as the back of the bow as a pressure board. Place the backing strip of wood onto the back of the bow. Cut a bicycle inner tube in half and then cut each half lengthwise in half again. You now have four long lengths of rubber stripping to bind the back of the bow to the backing strip. Place the dowel down the center of the backing strip and use the rubber strips to hold the dowel, backing strip and bow together by wrapping the entire lamination from tip to tip. Be sure that there is excess glue squeezing out of the joint along the entire length of the bow. This will assure a good, tight seal. Let the bow dry for at least a week before unwrapping or working the bow.

Once the bow is dry, use sandstone or sandpaper to clean the edges of the bow. Sand all of the joints well so there is only a thin lamination line showing. Sand or file the ends of the backing strip so that it fits neatly into the tips. If the strip is joined and sanded properly, the nocks will not need to be drastically cut again to fit the strip.

It is common to have to re-tiller the bow after the wood strip has been laid on so don't be concerned if the bow is not arching correctly. Simply use the tillering board and the plane to fit the bow round the tiller again. The draw weight of the bow may have exceeded the point desired, if so continue to work on the belly of the bow in the same manner as you did when first working the wood.

Wood backing makes for a very attractive bow, especially if a contrasting wood is used. A rawhide backing is superfluous at this time, unless a smooth and non-porous surface is desired for painting.

There are no examples of wooden backed bows from West of the Mississippi to this author's knowledge, so this could damage any traditional or historical value of the bow. One other problem with a wooden backed bow is that the backing strip will not adhere forever. Eventually the glue seal breaks and the entire bow usually breaks. If these problems do not bother you, then take heart as a wooden backed bow is quite nice and quick to shoot if the proper wood/backing combinations are used.

⌘ ⌘ ⌘

Rawhide has long been a favorite backing material in my lodge. It is tough, strong, and quite transparent if you want to place a color on the back of the bow under the rawhide layer. Rawhide can come from deer, elk, cow, horse or buffalo. None of these will increase the strength or cast of the bow, the main purpose of a rawhide backing being to protect the back of the bow from hard knocks and to keep splinters or hairs of wood or sinew from lifting or fracturing on the bow back. It is also the ideal surface to paint upon if a painted back is desired.

Rawhide may be obtained in many ways. You can either buy it at the local leather store, craft store or tannery, or you can make it yourself with a minimum of work. Rawhide is actually what the name implies: a raw, unfinished, untanned hide. All you need to do to make rawhide is stretch a skin on a hide frame and scrape it until all the flesh, fat and hairs have been removed. It does not make a difference whether it is scraped wet or dry. After the skin has been scraped, wash it with dish washing soap and water. Rinse it well so the rawhide does not smell.

Sometimes it is hard to find a piece of rawhide long enough to cover the bow from end to end, so you may have to use two shorter hides that meet in the center of the bow. Cut the rawhide one-half inch wider than the bow limb at its widest point. Don't worry about length too much as it will stretch when wet.

Once the rawhide is cut it should be placed in a bucket of warm water. Let it soak for five or six hours and while it is soaking, you can begin to make some hide glue.

Regardless of what you may have heard, nothing holds natural materials together as well as home made hide glue. You can purchase hide glue in liquid or powdered form at the local art store, but these glues are made from rabbit skin. They do work, but not as well as a good home made brew, and some of the old bowyers feel they lack *spirit* or authenticity. If you do use the prepared glues, make the following changes in their preparation: If the liquid form is used, mix two capfuls of white vinegar in each cup of liquid glue. This speeds the drying process as liquid hide glue can take two to three weeks to set. If the powdered form is used, mix the glue with half the amount of water recommended by the manufacturer. Always use a crock-pot or double boiler to make up the powdered glue, if possible.

One disadvantage of the home made brew is the unpleasant aroma it gives off during production.

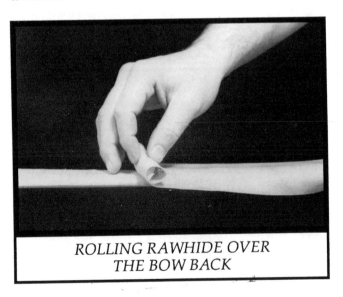

*ROLLING RAWHIDE OVER
THE BOW BACK*

TRADITIONAL HIDE GLUE

To make homemade glue you will need: (1) dewclaws from deer, elk or cow; (2) hide scraps, if available; (3) small chunks of rawhide; (4) scraps of brain-tanned leather, if available; (5) scrap sinew; (6) an old-style (iron) Dutch oven with a lid; and, (7) water. The brain-tanned hide scraps and the hide scraps are not necessary but they help the glue acquire a smooth consistency.

Place the necessary ingredients in any quantity into the Dutch oven. Pour enough water into the oven to cover all of the ingredients and put the lid on the pot. The lid keeps some of the *sticky* in the glue. Turn on the heat, either with charcoal or a stove. Boil this conglomerate for a few hours adding water occasionally to prevent the glue from drying out or over-cooking. The fastest time in which I produced glue was three and one-half hours.

The biggest mistake most craftsmen make when cooking hide glue is that they expect the ingredients to dissolve or melt in the pot. This is not the case. The protein in the ingredients simply cooks out into the water and the heat. Keep the water at or near a continual slow boil. The water will become thick, sticky and slightly stinky, but the ingredients will still be there when the glue is complete.

You may want to make more glue than you will need at this time so that you will have it in the future. Just add water to the glue in the pot and let it boil a little longer. To store the glue, place it in the freezer or allow it to dry out in a shallow pan or plate. It is easily reconstituted by adding water and re-heating for a while. The frozen glue will reconstitute quicker than the dry type, especially if you use a double boiler.

GLUE INGREDIENTS

Once the glue is made and the rawhide soaked, scrape the back of the bow with a saw blade. Make sure that the entire back is abraded from tip to tip. Wet down the back of the bow with warm water, and *paint* the back of the bow with hide glue. Get the glue along the sides of the bow as well as the back. Let this primer dry for a few minutes and then paint the back with glue again. This time, however, put the rawhide down as you paint the back. Quickly wrap

WRAPPING RAWHIDE WITH STRETCH GAUZE

either gauze or cheesecloth around the raw-hide and the belly to hold the rawhide in place until it dries. The rawhide will go over the belly by one-quarter inch, so be sure that you were liberal with the glue. Once it is wrapped, leave the bow in a cool, dry location for about a week. Unwrap the bow after this time, and you will have a nearly completed bow!

Use a fine, wide file at the edges of the bow to remove any excess rawhide on the belly. If you are careful, you can blend the rawhide into the wood on the belly so well that no one will be able to see or feel where the wood stops and the rawhide begins.

Once it has been filed, use linseed oil, bear grease, fat or plain lard from the grocery store to moisten the belly. Rub it in well (so that it shines) to keep the wood from drying out.

✠ ✠ ✠

Before describing how to make a *sinew backed* bow, let's look at what a sinew backing actually is. If a bow is made of wood, the application of sinew is called sinew *backing*. This is simply a sinew lining and should not be confused with the sinew back of a horn bow. The difference is that a wood bow can function on its own, without the aid of the sinew on the back; the sinew simply adds speed and strength to the bow. On the other hand, a horn bow cannot function without sinew on its back. Horn will withstand a great deal of compression, but it cannot accept tension. The sinew back of a horn bow is a real back, performing half of the duties of the limb.

In this bowyers opinion, sinew is far superior to other backing materials. It not only adds to the speed and cast of a bow, it can also increase the draw weight if desired. The thing I like best is that it is authentic and still makes for a very fast bow.

The rubber-like quality sinew exhibits in expansion and contraction makes it superior to even modern day fiberglass. Also, sinew never really cures or gets dry enough to break or crack. I have seen it split off a bow back due to

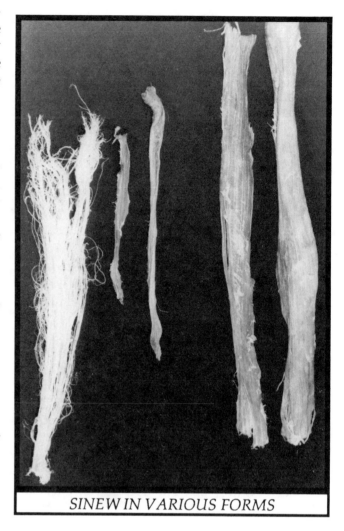

SINEW IN VARIOUS FORMS

a poor glue job, but it did not break whereas the bow limb did.

The first step is to obtain sinew in sufficient quantity. This may be difficult because meat packers and commodity houses are few and far between. Furthermore, most meat packers are reluctant to provide sinew as it spoils the cut of meat if they cut it off the loin. To get around this problem, find out what day they prepare hamburger and ask for some at that time. You need what the butcher calls the *silver skin* from the loin. Neck sinew or silver skin is not usable; you want back sinew whenever possible. You can obtain sinew for free by cutting it out of legs the packing house throws away, but leg sinew will not break up as fine as back sinew. Leg sinew is also shorter and there is less of it; however, you can use leg sinew if nothing else is available. Some bowyers feel that leg sinew

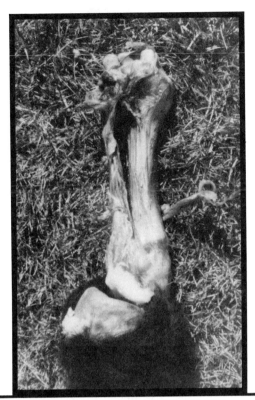

LEG SINEW ON THE HOOF

FLORIST'S FROG

the sinew into quarter-inch wide strips. From here, tease or break the strips into fine threads in one of two ways: (1) Clamp a *florists frog* in a vise and drag the strips through the teeth. Use a length of wood to press the sinew into the nails of the frog and then pull until the sinew strands take on a feathery appearance. (2) The other method is to clamp a curry comb in a vise and treat the sinew in the same way as with the frog.

As long as the sinew is shredded to the point where it looks feathered, the method used does not matter; the end product is what counts. Some old bowyers went so far as to chew the

is stronger than back sinew but most bowyers, including myself, disagree.

Once you find a supply of sinew, hoard it; get as much of it as you can; lie about it to your friends; and, find other sources! Sinew is as scarce as gold these days although, if you don't mind paying high prices, there are a few places that sell sinew already cut, cleaned and dried. Buffalo, deer, elk, cow, horse and moose are all sources of backing sinew but I have found that buffalo and elk are the best, with horse and deer following close behind. Sinew from the other animals listed works well, it just takes twice as much.

If you get raw or fresh sinew, use a dull knife to scrape the meat and fat off the sinew strap; this reduces the grease. Wash it at this point if you wish, then let it dry in thin, flat strips on a wire rack or board.

When the strips have reached a hard, semi-lucent (shiny) state, twist or jerk them to break the sinew out of the tissue that covers it. Tear

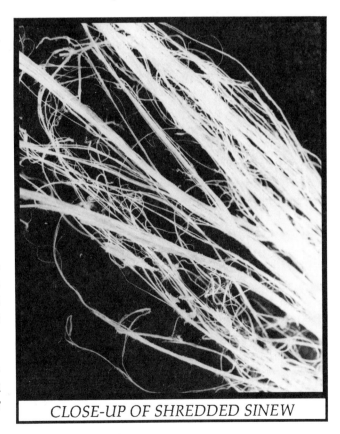

CLOSE-UP OF SHREDDED SINEW

sinew to get the desired consistency. I did this with my second bow to see if I could make a bow using only the oldest methods, using no tools at all. The sinew didn't taste too bad at first, but after chewing 200 bundles of un-washed sinew in one afternoon, I was ready to quit.

In recent years, a few bowyers have advocated pounding the sinew with a hammer or rawhide mallet, with the sinew resting on rock or con-crete. I find it hard to believe that these bowyers have ever made a primitive bow much less one of any quality. Using a hammer on a hard surface will cut the sinew into short, unusable junk. Sinew can be cut or broken, but never pulled in half; not even in a one or two strand quantity.

Forming the sinew into a threaded or finely shredded state is the entire secret to making a high quality backed bow. This is why the frog or curry comb methods will work so well. Do not try to make the process go faster by short changing yourself at this stage. Getting the sinew ready is the most important part of back-ing a bow.

Take a bunch of feathered sinew strands in your hand and make a bundle as big around as a pencil. Use a scrap piece of sinew to tie these strands together. Form all the sinew you have into bundles. A strong, heavy sinew backing will require two or three hundred bundles. If only the back is to be covered with sinew, seventy-five to one hundred bundles should be enough. You may skip the bundling of the sinew if you wish, but having the sinew in packages will save time.

While you are making the sinew bundles, it is a good idea to start the hide glue cooking (the recipe for hide glue is found earlier in this Chapter). Make a lot more than you made before, as backing with sinew requires a great deal of glue. I know of no other glue that can be used in this process. Dr. Grayson of Klatskanie, Oregon has used LePages liquid glue with some success, but I don't know his secret. As far as I know, no modern glue will work with sinew and artificial sinew cannot be used to

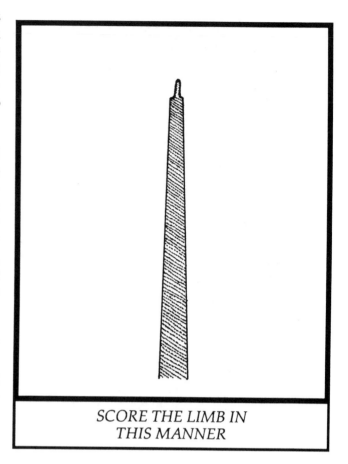

SCORE THE LIMB IN
THIS MANNER

back a bow.

✠ ✠ ✠

After making the sinew bundles and with the glue nearly ready, you will need to prepare the wood. Scrape the back of the bow with a rough file or the blade of a saw, going from tip to tip to raise the nap of the wood. If you have used Osage orange, juniper or any other oily hard-wood, you will need to wash down the back with a ten percent mixture of lye and water. Use steel wool or rawhide to rub the back

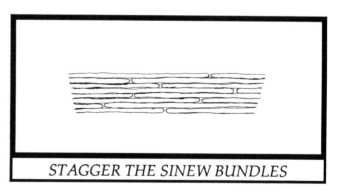

STAGGER THE SINEW BUNDLES

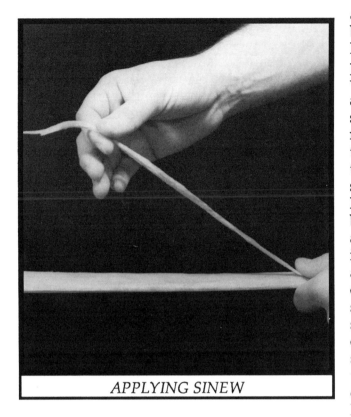

APPLYING SINEW

down, rinse with white vinegar and let it dry.

✠ ✠ ✠

Now that the sinew is ready, the glue is done and the bow is prepared, you can proceed with placing sinew on the back. Place a few sinew bundles in a sink of warm water. Do not use hot water as the sinew will turn to elastic string. Let the sinew get soggy and limp, and test the glue to make sure it is not too hot for the sinew. Place the bow in a vise or clamp at the handle and paint the glue down the entire length of the back. Let this get tacky. It helps at this point to have the sinew bundles divided into two equal piles. Take a soggy bundle of sinew out of the water and put it into the glue. Swish it around and take it back out. Pull the sticky strand of sinew between your thumb and forefinger to remove any excess glue and, at the same time, take off the strand you used to tie the bundle together. Put the sinew on the back of the bow starting at one tip. Wrap over the nock by at least an inch. Use your finger to smooth out the bundle, stroking it slowly so that it will lie flat and thin across the back. Put another bundle into the glue, remove the tie and excess glue, and place it next to the last bundle. Smooth this out as you did the first one. As you lay the sinew bundles on the back, stagger the lengths so that none of the ends are in line with each other (see illustration); this will assure a strong seal. Continue to lay the sinew over the back in this fashion until the entire limb has been covered. Now, starting at the other tip, do the other limb the same way with the sinew overlapping at the handles. Use the same number of bundles on the second limb as you used on the first. If you place the sinew on the limbs evenly and in equal amounts at this point, you will save yourself a lot of grief and effort by not having to re-tiller the bow after the sinew is in place.

Use additional layers as you wish, but keep in mind that more sinew means more draw weight. As you place more layers on the bow, build the middle of the back higher so that the

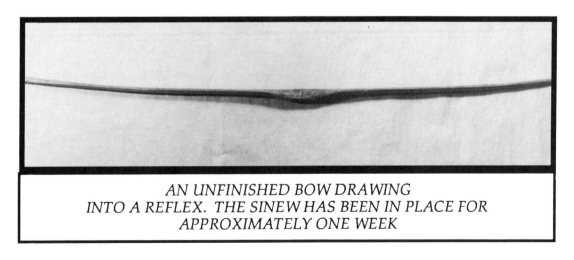

AN UNFINISHED BOW DRAWING
INTO A REFLEX. THE SINEW HAS BEEN IN PLACE FOR
APPROXIMATELY ONE WEEK

sinew tapers on both sides towards the edges of the bow. If you plan to place more than a quarter of an inch (when dried) of sinew on the back, you will need to wrap gauze over the first sinew layer. Keep in mind that a quarter inch of dry sinew is about equal to one-half inch of wet sinew. If you must wrap the sinew with gauze, take the gauze off and reverse the direction of the wrap every twelve hours. If this is not done you will have bandage marks in the sinew.

☒ ☒ ☒

Allow the finished back to dry for at least one month in the summer and three to four months in the winter. Don't get impatient and string the bow early. To quote an old friend, "Time wounds all heels." It will take between nine months and a year, or more, for the sinew to cure properly. It is safe to shoot the bow, if you wish, after this amount of time has passed. It is almost certain that, while Turkish bowyers waited five to six years for their bows to cure, the Lakotah people hunted with theirs in five to six months. Gall, a famous Lakotah archer, once said that it took "five moons or more" to make a good and powerful bow.

After the sinew has dried or cured for long enough to drive you crazy, string the bow and slowly draw it half way. Check the tiller again; if you laid the sinew properly it will draw correctly. If it is a bit out of round, file or scrape the belly until it comes *round the tiller*. Be sure to work only on the belly. One bowyer recently suggested filing down the sinew to tiller the bow - if you do this, you will spoil a lot of hard work. All you will do is peel the sinew where it is in short pieces.

☒ ☒ ☒

Two final points: Sinew, as it dries, will draw the limbs into a slight reflex. This will continue for about a year or even more, so don't be alarmed if the limbs slightly reverse. Secondly, you can have too much sinew on the back and the amount varies with the hardness of different woods. A good rule of thumb is to never use more thickness of sinew than you have thickness of wood. If the sinew is too thick, it will throw too much compression upon the belly and the bow will split or crack. Eventually, the limb will snap at the maximum point of compression.

FINISH WORK

To many, finishing the bow is the most enjoyable part. When you show your friends the final product, it should look great as well as shoot great. The type of bow you have crafted will help determine the way it is finished.

Most Plains bows were self bows until the mid-1800s, so there were few with sinew to cover, rawhide to paint, or snake skin to clean. Many of them were not even painted. Only the greatest hunters or warriors had painted or sinew backed bows; usually the entire bow was simply warmed and rubbed over with a mixture of brains and lard. If you choose to finish your bow in this manner, simply go to your local butcher or stockyard and get some brains and hard white fat. Place the brains in a blender and mix until liquified. Heat the fat in a pan until it too is liquid. Pour the brains into the pot with the fat and blend well, then allow the mixture to cool just enough that it will not burn your hand. Use a natural sponge or, better yet, a bit of tanned hide and rub the mixture into the bow. Be sure the bow is warm but not hot when you rub in the blend. Then allow the bow to cool and rub it with dry buckskin until you have a high luster.

Although this is the oldest way to finish a bow, it certainly isn't the only way. It definitely helps any bow to have the belly prepared this way once it is ready to shoot.

✠ ✠ ✠

A bow that is sinew backed may be finished any number of ways. The first, and probably the oldest method, is to *paint* colored earths such as ochre, charcoal or red clay over the back as the sinew is laid on. These may also have been mixed with the glue to achieve a more distinct color. Putting the color into the sinew as it is laid on, creates a permanent, non-fading

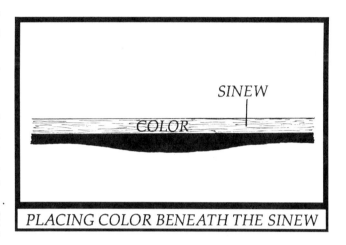

PLACING COLOR BENEATH THE SINEW

finish. You can even use powdered paints to match this effect. Painting does not protect the sinew from moisture or bumps which, I believe, is why this method did not last long. At the same time, if you use this method and do not care for the results, it is a simple task to put on a different color.

Quite a few Northwestern and Western bows have sinew backs with a rawhide or small intestine covering. Most of the Modoc/Yana bows in later years (1850 on) were also rawhide or intestine covered, even if they were not sinew or wood backed. The covering provides protection from moisture (particularly important with a sinew backed bow) and from damage done by hitting the bow against other objects. It also affords a good medium on which to paint.

Rawhide is a good covering material and it is easy to find. You can make it yourself in a couple of hours or you can run down to the local leather or craft shop and buy some. Either way, it works the same. Rawhide should be cut one-half inch wider than the bow limbs to be covered.

Intestines, on the other hand, cannot be purchased, so you will need to find a slaughterhouse that is willing to let you cut four or five feet from their commodity barrels; most of them are happy to let you. During the hunting season, deer intestine is available and actually works better than cow's intestine as it seems to dry a bit harder. Elk will also work well, so use whatever you can find.

The application of rawhide or intestine is the same. Place the rawhide or intestine in a tub of warm water and allow it to soak until it is completely saturated and limp. While the rawhide or intestine is soaking, make or reconstitute some hide glue; make it thick for this purpose. If you are using rawhide, roll the strip into a cylinder with the flesh side out. Use a rubber band to hold it in this form and place it back in the water until you are ready to use it. Put the bow in a vise, clamping at the handle and paint a layer of warm glue down the back. If you are using intestine, paint the belly and handle at the same time. Let this coat of glue get tacky. Remove the rawhide or intestine from the water. Paint three or four inches from one tip with glue and unroll the rawhide the same distance. With intestines, pull it down over the back and belly as far as they have been painted with glue. Continue painting the glue ahead of the covering as you roll it out, or pull it down, until you have reached the other tip of the bow. With intestine, it is a good idea to work in a very warm and humid room. Work fast as it is not easy to pull the whole length of intestine at once and you will need to pull it down in stages much as you would put on a pair of tight jeans. Be liberal with the glue as you have only one chance and must finish before the glue begins to dry.

✠ ✠ ✠

Once the covering is in place, use gauze or cloth strips to tightly wrap the entire bow. Take the wraps off and reverse their directions approximately every twenty-four hours for a week. Doing this avoids making marks on the rawhide or intestine. The covering will be semiclear and very hard in approximately two weeks. If you have used rawhide, take a file to the edges of the weapon and blend the rawhide into the wood. If you are careful with the file, no one will be able to see where the rawhide ends and the wood begins.

You may now consider the bow finished if you so desire. However, the belly and handle may still be finished and adding a sinew wrap just below the nocks adds a nice touch. You may also want to paint the bow a solid color or with a design. California bows are especially well known for their colors and designs. Most of the Modoc/Yana types were done with reds and blacks, but some yellows and blacks have been noted. You may also want to wrap sinew around the nocks with horsehair under it as a pendant. There are dozens of ways to finish bow limbs and you should do some research and use the technique you like best.

✠ ✠ ✠

I have saved the snake skin back until last, as a bow covered with snake skin was considered by some tribes to be the "ultimate"; fewer than one in ten were backed with snake skin, and these few are of the finest manufacture. As a matter of fact, a good snake skin covered, sinew backed bow was once worth two horses. A snake skin lends a very business-like attitude

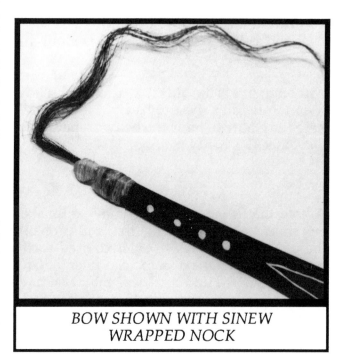

BOW SHOWN WITH SINEW WRAPPED NOCK

CALIFORNIA PAINTED BOWS

43

to any bow, sheds water and also acts as natural camouflage. Many 1865-1885 bows were covered with snake skin, which makes it a very authentic covering. It also happens to be a personal favorite of the author.

as performance is concerned. A tanned skin does have more luster than a raw skin and the untanned variety has a tendency to lose more scales.

✠ ✠ ✠

Cut the skins to length so that they meet at the same point on the handle. The head end of the skin should be at the handle and the ends should slightly overlap the nocks. If you have used a single skin you will need to cut it in half so that the scales run in opposite directions on the respective limbs. The scales should appear to be going toward the tips. Cut the width of the skins one and three-quarters times the width of the limb to be covered. Place the skins in warm water to soak.

You will again need hide glue, so make some up while the skins are soaking. Make the glue just a little thinner than what was suggested for other applications.

✠ ✠ ✠

Note: Although it is entirely up to you, it is a good idea to lay rawhide over the sinew before gluing snake skin on the back. Never lay snake directly over bare wood if the bow does not have sinew backing. The rawhide will give a smooth surface upon which to glue and will prevent wood or sinew *splinters* from rising or popping through the snake skin.

*BOW THAT HAS BEEN
SNAKESKIN COVERED*

Securing skins is not at all a difficult task. Finding two that match well, however, is a bit more of a chore. You may, of course, use one skin if you can find one long enough to cover both limbs. Whatever skins you use, they must be flawless and without holes or tears. Note: Be sure and check your local and state laws before acquiring snake skin as many snakes are protected by law.

Some have purported that the skin must be raw (untanned) for use on a bow. Others have said that the skin must be tanned in order to flex properly. Having used both, there seems to be no noticeable difference between the two as far

✠ ✠ ✠

While the skin is warm and wet, roll it up flesh side out and tail to end. If rattlesnake skins are used, remove the rattles prior to this stage as they fall off after a few shots and besides, they make noise. *Again*, before using these or any other snake skin, check with your local wildlife department to make sure they are not protected by law.

Paint glue on one limb of the bow from the handle to the tip; let this coat get tacky, but not too dry (about five minutes will be fine). Then, paint glue four or five inches, and roll the same

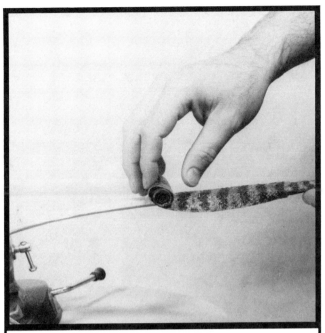

ROLLING SNAKESKIN ON THE
BACK OF THE BOW

WRAPPING THE COVERED LIMB
WITH GAUZE

amount of skin, down from the tip. Brush glue a few inches ahead of the skin as you unroll it until you reach the handle. Now turn the bow around and apply the skin to the other limb in the same manner. If you try to save time or energy by painting the entire limb at once, you will find that the skin will tear if you have to change its position. Also, the sides will absorb the glue and the skin won't stick properly where you need it most. Learn from my mistakes and make a better bow.

⊞ ⊞ ⊞

Wrap gauze or strips of linen around the limbs and let the skin dry for a week. Remove the gauze slowly so the edge of the skin is not caught and ripped. Use a sharp razor blade to cut the excess skin off the limb; a strip of masking tape can help guide the blade. Cut off any overlap of skin at the handle and then use a stiff brush to remove any loose scales. Scales will fly the first time you draw the bow if you don't get the loose ones at this stage.

Using snake skin requires the ends of the limbs,

below the nocks, to be bound with sinew, rawhide or wound leather. Without binding at the nocks, the bow string will quickly strip off the skin. Sinew wraps nicely or wet rawhide can be sewn into place. Do whatever appeals to you.

⊞ ⊞ ⊞

There is one more material known to have been used as a bow back covering, but examples of it are extremely rare and only occur after contact with the white man. Some of the bows in the Smithsonian and in the Museum of the American Indian have canvas in place of rawhide or snake skin. These are not painted or decorated in any way, but for the sake of thoroughness, I felt it should be mentioned here.

⊞ ⊞ ⊞

Finishing the belly of the bow is completely different from finishing the back. You look at the belly as you shoot, so you do not want anything too distracting. You may want to simply grease the natural wood and let it go at that. This is probably the most authentic finish

45

NOCK WITH HORSE HAIR
PENDANT ADDED

anyway.

Painting the belly is my preferred finish. A solid color is very nice, with perhaps a thin line from tip to tip. I recently finished one bow by painting the entire belly with fresh cow's blood; I even painted the leather handle. After it has dried for a week or so, the blood takes on a very pleasing reddish-brown color that appears very old. Blood also makes a very old looking bow out of a self bow. Just paint the entire bow, back and belly, tip to tip with blood. Blood, of course, is available at any time from any slaughterhouse.

Intricate belly designs are uncommon on old bows, but certainly do exist. Bows with complicated belly designs or paint were usually made after 1870 and during the reservation period. The painting on Plains bow bellies is rarely geometric as women did not paint bows. Only men were allowed to handle a hunter's or warrior's bow, which probably accounts for the shabby way in which many of them are finished.

✠ ✠ ✠

Note: Should you decide to paint the belly or back, try to avoid a heavy concentration of black paint, particularly on the belly. Black will absorb heat and may cause the limbs to become brittle. A very thin black, with a great deal of fat or grease rubbed over it, should be alright.

✠ ✠ ✠

The handle can also be finished any number of ways. Wet rawhide can be sewn around the grip for a solid look. Use a baseball stitch to sew it on and have the seam at the back of the bow for comfort.

Trade cloth makes a nice handle whether it is wrapped or sewn. Trade cloth or wool has been a trade item on the Plains since the days of the Lewis and Clarke expedition in 1803. The cloth used for bow handles was usually a remnant of a worn garment or what was left over after a woman boiled the cloth to obtain dye for quills. A bit of buckskin wrapped at the top and

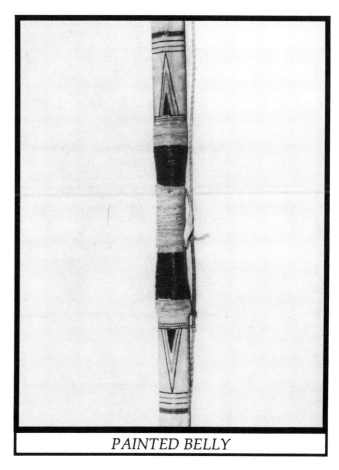

PAINTED BELLY

bottom of the cloth adds a nice contrast. Better still is a touch of quillwork or beadwork on the handle.

There are quite a few examples of old bows with dyed buckskin handles; Catlin specifically mentions ochre and red. The bows seen in museums are generally too sweat-stained or greased to know what color they were originally. Buckskin handles are quite attractive and authentic, as well as being easy to produce.

✠ ✠ ✠

Fur handles are not desirable as they make your hand sweat and eventually the skin rots. Fur will also drastically affect the arrow's flight if it has not been applied properly to the grip. There are, however, a number of bows with fur above and below the handles for decorative purposes. Bodmer's painting of a Hidatsa Dog Dancer shows him holding a horn bow with fur wrapped about the mid-limb. Catlin shows

47

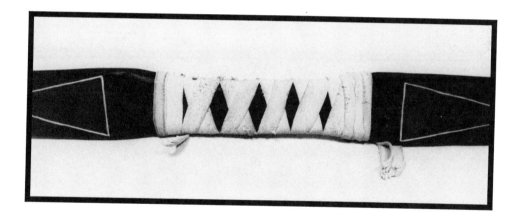

hunters with fur tied to the string, but logic suggests that this was a primitive silencer.

Many handles, particularly on bows with rawhide backs, are simply painted. California bows are well known for painted designs that seem to start at the handle and work their way out to the tips.

Once again, how you finish your bow is up to you. These are simply suggestions to help the first time bowyer decide which finish to use. My only other suggestion would be to finish the bow in an authentic manner. You have, by this time, created a beautiful, traditional work of art and craftsmanship and it would be sad if you were to finish it with cheap parodies of

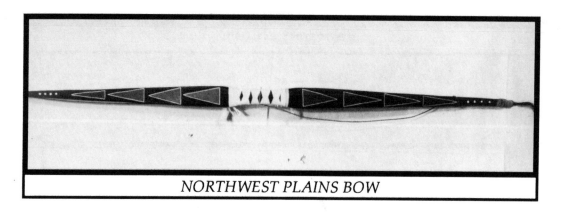
NORTHWEST PLAINS BOW

Native American design. For example, a "thunderbird" would not be appropriate. There are hundreds of photographs and drawings in books and museums which can be studied for ideas and there are a number of good examples in this book.

✠ ✠ ✠

A fine bow was once a symbol of passage from boyhood to manhood and men were very proud of their bows; they liked to show them off among themselves and other tribes. Make something of which you will be proud. All the sinew and snake skin back in the world cannot make up for a bad paint job or Hollywood designs!

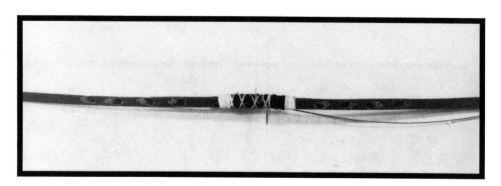

BOWSTRINGS

The bowstring is probably the most overlooked, ignored piece of any archer's tackle. I find this surprising as the bowstring is as integral to a bow as the engine is to a car. Perhaps this is because, like an engine, we expect it to always provide good and faithful service. A good string will just about do that, depending on the amount of shooting you do. On the other hand, a weak string or one that stretches will give you nothing but headaches. A poor string can even be responsible for poor accuracy or a broken bow, so plan at the start to obtain a bowstring of high quality.

Bowstrings can be made from many different materials, so whether you are a purist or an adventurous Scouter, there is a string for you. Sinew, cotton, linen, artificial sinew, under-bark, and nylon all make great strings. Every archer should at least try making a bowstring, if only because it gives you another reason to work with your bow. It will also give you a sense of accomplishment to make a string that fits the bow you have manufactured.

⌘ ⌘ ⌘

For the purist or traditionalist, sinew and under-bark are the only two choices. The under-bark is actually the cambium layer of the tree. Cottonwood, oak, ash, cherry, or walnut are just a few of the woods that will work. The cambium is stripped out and twisted in much the same way as you would use to make a rope. Although I have made several small ropes using natural plant fiber, I have never made a bowstring of twisted fiber. There are, however, a number of good books on the subject. At the same time, it is important to note that the Plains and California tribes generally used sinew for bowstrings.

Sinew strings are as traditionally correct as can

be managed. A good sinew string can support the weight of two pickup trucks even though it may be only three-sixteenths of an inch thick. The only drawback to a sinew string is that it cannot be used in an area of high humidity or in the rain; a damp sinew string will either stretch or break. This is why the Indians did not like it when soldiers wanted to fight in the rain. American Eagle, a well-known Lakotah warrior, said "he could throw a stone farther than the wet bow could throw the arrow." If you desire a sinew string, do not hunt or fight in the rain.

As mentioned before, obtaining sinew is the most difficult part of any project. Once in hand, sinew works well and is readily turned into a string. You will need three or four back straps, or five to six leg sinews for one string. Make sure the sinew is as long as possible.

Twist and tear the dry sinew to remove the outer tissue. Shred the sinew as best you can; you want to achieve a *feathery* appearance. Use a *florists frog* to shred if necessary. Have a bucket of warm water handy. The water must be cool enough to keep your hand in it or the sinew will turn to rubber.

Make bundles of sinew that are about one-eighth of an inch in diameter. Cut off any stiff, unbreakable bits of tissue on the ends of the bundles. Don't "square off" the ends of the bundles as the twist holds better if the ends are slightly uneven.

Place a couple of the bundles in the pan of water for a few minutes. When they become limp, place one end of the first bundle in a vise or even between your toes. Make sure that the end will be held firmly. Begin twisting the wet sinew about one inch from the attached end and slowly twist down the strand. When you

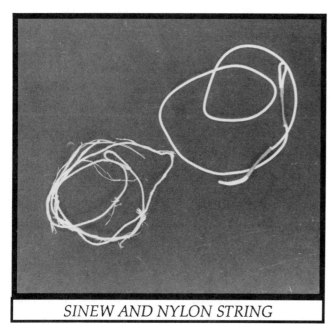

SINEW AND NYLON STRING

are about three-fourths of the way down the strand, put more sinew in the water and remove the soaked bundles. Begin to splice this into the free end of the sinew and continue to twist. Do not twist so hard that the strand begins to kink.

Keep adding sinew to the cord as you twist. Move rapidly so that the sinew doesn't get too dry but not so fast that you don't get a good splice. You may need to splash water on the string occasionally to keep it limber. Incidentally, if you are using your feet, you will have to wind the string around your free foot when it reaches about four feet in length. Four hands would really help during this process.

Once the cord has reached a length at least two and a half times as long as your bow (a four foot bow equals a ten foot cord), fold the twisted cord in half in such a way that none of the splices are next to each other. If you do get a splice on top of another splice, your string will not be as strong as it could be.

Begin to twist the doubled strand in the <u>opposite direction</u> from the way you twisted the single strand. Continue to twist until the cord begins to kink. As you twist the string, be sure that the tension on both strands is equal. I usually shove a stick or dowel in the doubled

end and use it to twist and pull at the same time; this gives a better grip than simply using two fingers. Don't pull the string too hard at this point, but do find a weight that is heavy enough to pull the string straight until it is dry (a shoe sometimes works well). Don't tie the cord in such a way that it can untwist as it dries. You may even want to sit by the fire and hold one end in your fingers and the other end in your toes until it dries. In any event, keep the tension on the string constant.

✠ ✠ ✠

After the string is dry, you may want to use fingernail clippers to remove unwanted *hairs* from the sinew. You may also wish to put a loop or slip-knot in one end of the string. The Plains Indians did not do this, they simply tied the string permanently to one end of the bow or sometimes had a hole the string was passed through and then knotted. They nearly always tied the free end to brace the bow. In later years (post 1860) some tribes began to use a noose on the free end.

Before using the string on the bow, hold one end in each hand and pull on it. The string should have very little stretch. After the string is put on the bow it will stretch for awhile, but it will settle down unless it is humid or damp. If the string will withstand your pulling on it at this point, it should work just fine on the bow. If it breaks, thank heaven that it happened now and not on the bow. If it does break, try again.

Some people claim you should coat the string with hide glue. I have never done this, nor have any of the old-time bowyers. No historical account says anything about this and it doesn't really make sense as repeated shooting would cause the glue to flake off the string. It may also slow down the reflex of the string. In any event, it seems to be more of a hindrance than a help.

✠ ✠ ✠

Artificial sinew seems to be a good compromise between tradition and practicality. It only stretches for a day or so, you can use it in the rain and, best of all, it looks very real. In fact,

*USING A DRILL AND HOOK TO TWIST
ARTIFICIAL SINEW*

you cannot tell the difference between a used, real sinew string and an artificial sinew string unless they are right next to each other.

To make a string of artificial sinew you will need a thirty foot length of sinew, a clamp or vise, a reversible drill and a cup hook. Double the sinew so that you have one length that has

two strands and is fifteen feet long. Clamp the two ends to a table or in the vise. Place the cup hook in the chuck of the drill, hook the free end of the sinew into the curl of the cup hook, then step back and pull the cord tight. Use the drill to twist the cord to the right. Twist until it begins to kink.

Remove the sinew from the cup hook, but do not allow it to untwist. Now divide the cord in half and place the new-found middle in the cup hook. Clamp the other end in the vise with the original ends. This will give you a cord that is roughly seven feet in length. Begin to twist the cord again, only this time twist the string to the left or <u>opposite</u> the original twist. Twist until the string begins to develop kinks.

Use a scrap of leather to rub the length of the string before removing it from the clamp. Rubbing will fix the wax into the strands and keep it from untwisting. Remove the string from the clamp and drill and cut off any frayed edges that developed in the vise. You now have a practical, near-authentic bowstring.

A third kind of string you can make is called a *running line* string, and it is nearly the same as the type you buy from a sporting goods store. While it is completely contemporary, it is very easy to make. Waxed cotton, linen, artificial sinew, or even dental floss will work well for this kind of string.

*DIVIDING THE STRING
IN HALF*

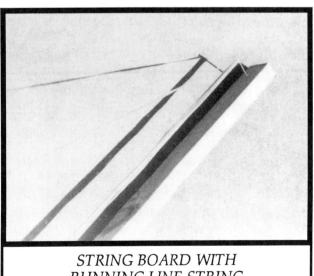

*STRING BOARD WITH
RUNNING LINE STRING*

You will need a *string board* in order to start. This is simply a board at least one foot longer than the bow you've made with a nail in the top of each end. Tie one end of your roll of string to one of the nails, leaving a tail five feet long behind the knot. Now begin to go around the outside of both nails in a clockwise direction. You will need six winds for bows from thirty to fifty pounds. Anything over fifty pounds will require eight to ten winds.

After the winds are complete, cut the line from the spool, leaving about a foot to spare. Now untie the end with the tail and bring it around the nail it was tied to and down the board so that it is just below the opposite nail. Tie this strand to the ending strand about three inches below the nail. Make the ties so that the main body of the string is inside of the knot. This will keep the string cords at an even length.

Cut off the shorter strand to about a two inch length. Grasp the longer free strand and tie a series of half hitches starting below the knot and going over and beyond it, until you are about one and one-half inches from the nail. There are an equal number of strands on either side of the nail. Begin tying another series of half hitches, but this time catch only the strands on one side of the nail. Continue to tie these knots around the nail until you meet up with the knots on the main body of the string. You now have a loop in one end of your string.

On the other end of the string, tie a length of scrap cord around the strands four inches from the nail. Use half hitches around all of the strands to whip the end of the string. Remove the string from the board and tie the loop-less end to the bottom bow limb so that the noose is about four inches below the top nock.

✠ ✠ ✠

To string the bow, place the tied end against the outside of your foot and press the opposite knee against the handle (belly side). Push with your hand on the top limb and your knee at the handle and bring the string over the nock. <u>**Never**</u> <u>step through</u> the string of a short bow! The limbs may twist resulting in serious injury

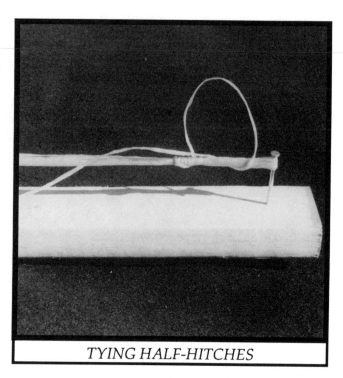

TYING HALF-HITCHES

to the bow. Once the string is on the bow, you can leave it there whether or not the bow is braced. Just slip the loop below the nock when the bow is relaxed.

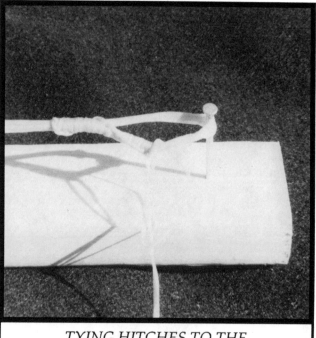

TYING HITCHES TO THE NOCK LOOP IN THE END OF THE STRING

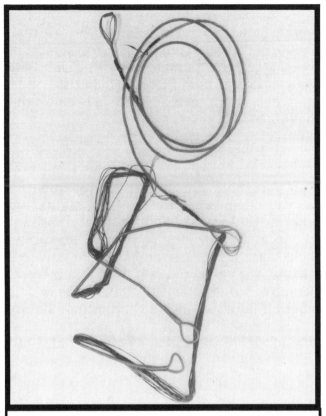

SHOWN ABOVE ARE ARTIFICAL SINEW AND COMMERCIALLY WOUND BOWSTRINGS

PROPER WAY TO BRACE OR STRING A BOW

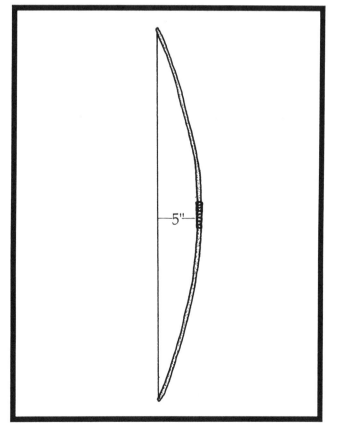

There is an alternative to this method of bow stringing. Put the loop over the top nock and down the bow about four inches. Now tie the free end to the other nock. Place the tied end against your foot with the back of the bow facing you this time. With one hand, grasp the bow around the top of the handle, keeping your elbow close to your body. Put the palm of your other hand on the back of the upper limb in such a way that the thumb and forefinger are free to slide the string up the limb as you pull the handle. Start the pull toward you as you push with the other hand on the upper limb. Slide the string into the nock. Be sure that it settles properly into the grooves cut for the string and then slowly bring the handle back into position. You are now ready to shoot.

As noted above, **do not** step through the bow. This obsolete method of stringing has twisted many limbs and caused bows to break. If you are intimidated by either of the methods above, go to the local sporting goods store and buy a bow stringer. They are very inexpensive and easy to use.

Just how high should the string be off of the bow? In other words, what should the distance be between the string and the handle when the bow is strung? The British use a measurement called a *fistmele*. This is the measurement of the fist plus the outstretched thumb. This works well for the English and their longbows, but the Plains and California Indian bows require only four to five inches between the center of the bow handle and the string. If the string is too high off of the riser or handle, the bow will not be able to shoot at its full potential. On the other hand, if the string is too low when braced, the string will not put enough resistance on the limbs when the arrow is fired causing the limbs to come back upon themselves. This can severely damage or break a limb. If you are really concerned about having the string at a proper height, use the fistmele method. Unless the bow is longer than fifty-six inches it will not give maximum service, but this is better than having a broken bow.

✠ ✠ ✠

Just remember, the bow string is as important as any other tackle for the bow, so make an effort to find or make a good one. If all else fails, the local archery supply shop will be able to help you. Make sure and take the bow to be strung with you or they won't know what length of string you need. The string should be about four or five inches shorter than the bow.

ARROWS

Ishi once said, "Any old stick him do for bow, but arrows kill deer." Arrows are works of art and arrows are important.

✠ ✠ ✠

There are two ways to make arrows: First is the white man method which is to split a round log into squares and then whittle the wood back into round shapes again. Second is the Indian way which is finding straight natural shafts. Either way, the objective is the same. We want a shaft that is straight, free of knots and strong. I have never tried the contemporary method as it seems slow, is less than perfect without machines and lacks the spirit of tradition, so we will forego any discussion of this method.

The Indian way is to choose straight shoots of first growth wood. Wild rose, willow, dogwood, wild plum, witch hazel, river reed, choke cherry, tamarack, currant and wild cherry are all good woods for arrow shafts. Some are better than others, but all will work. Chestnut trees that have blown over usually generate second growth shoots. These have no knots and are straight and strong.

Although the wood you choose will depend on the part of the country you live in, I have listed enough types to give anyone two or three choices. Keep an eye out for shaft materials during your travels. The shaft that killed my first buffalo was cut from a stand of wild rose found in the middle of an amusement park. Make sure and look along river bottoms, on heavily wooded mountain sides and in dark clearings. Once you become conscious of it, you will find shaft material all over the place. A burned out vacant lot recently yielded 200 to 300 shafts.

Personally, I prefer to use wild rose shoots:

they are almost perfectly straight, very dense, taper slowly and have great *spine* (they are "stiffer" than a different wood of an equal diameter). An arrow with too much spine will shoot to the left; conversely, an arrow with too little spine will shoot to the right. The amount of spine needed depends on the draw weight of the bow. With a bit of work, practice and experience you can develop small arrows that will shoot with more power from your short bow than is possible from a larger bow with unmatched arrows.

✠ ✠ ✠

Once you have found shafts to use, cut them. Cut as many as you can, but do not totally

*WILD SHAFTS GROWING ALONG SIDE
A MOUNTAIN ROAD*

deplete the area of growth as it is a good idea to leave some to grow next year. I try to bring home fifty to sixty shafts each time I go out and this will yield approximately thirty-five arrows. While it is best to cut shafts from November through April, you may cut them in the spring and hot months. Those cut in the winter will contain less moisture and are less apt to crack or split. If you cut shafts in the summer, do not dry them in the sun; keep them in the shade and turn them each morning as this will help dry them straight. It also works well to bundle twelve or eighteen shafts with lots of string or rubber bands and hang them in your garage to dry.

✠ ✠ ✠

Once the shafts are dry, you will need to strip or scrape off the bark. If you use willow or witch

CUT SHAFTS READY FOR BUNDLING

hazel, you may strip off the bark prior to drying the shaft. A sharp piece of obsidian or a knife blade works well for scraping the shaft as you want to clean down to white wood.

The next step is to cut the shafts down to size. The traditional method requires that you hold the shaft horizontally and place one end against your sternum or breast bone with the other end in your outstretched fingertips. The shaft should be cut where it reaches the end of your fingertips.

✠ ✠ ✠

Some archers suggest that the Indian method was to measure from the elbow to the end of the index finger plus one finger's length. This is a correct method but will only work if you have used the Indian way to determine bow size. My

CLOSE-UP OF NATURAL SHAFTS

58

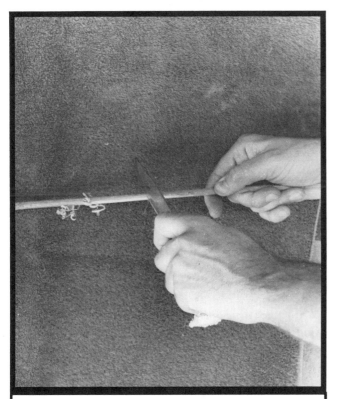

SCRAPING BARK OFF TO PREPARE THE SHAFT FOR STRAIGHTENING

SHAFT WRENCH WITH GROOVER

reach is twenty-five inches, but the average seems to be twenty-seven to twenty-eight inches. There is one exception to this rule of measurement: If you have a short bow, **be sure that the arrow length is no more than half the length of the bow!** For example, a forty-eight inch bow would draw up to a twenty-four inch arrow. Correct arrow length may not even be half the length of the bow, so know when the bow is *stacking up* or near fatal stress. Remember, a full drawn bow is seven-eighths broken. Never over-draw a primitive bow.

Next, the shafts need to be sorted according to spine, which is done by bending them. Hold the shafts by the ends and, press with your thumbs in the middle of the shaft to bend them. Group them in piles of shafts that bend the same way. Then, take a bunch of those that have been sorted and check them for straightness. If all went well during the drying stage, this should be easy. If not, you will need to use an arrow wrench, like the one illustrated, or you will need to straighten them with heat. I

suggest both methods in tandem.

Now identify the butt (large) end of the shaft. This is where the nock is cut with the smaller end taking an arrow head at a later stage. The cut of the nock will depend on the release you utilize. If you use the Mediterranean release (most common), you will have to cut deep nocks and bind them to prevent splitting. If you prefer using a pinch or secondary draw, the nock is flared and cut with a small file leaving only a small notch. Some of the arrows exhibited in museums have an "X" nock.

True Plains and Western arrows have enlarged nocks. This is necessary if you are shooting a

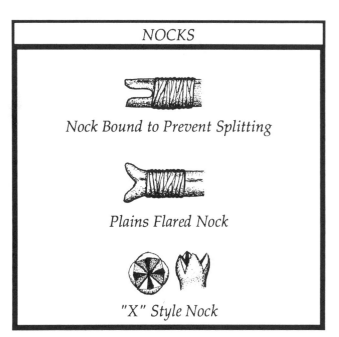

NOCKS

Nock Bound to Prevent Splitting

Plains Flared Nock

"X" Style Nock

true pinch (*primary*) or assisted pinch (*secondary* or *tertiary*) release. Enlarged nocks also help recess the binding on the *fletching* (or feathers) and improve the balance of the arrow. Decide on the type of nock and cut it. You may wish to slightly burn the nock to further harden the wood.

If you are making Indian-style arrows, you need to score or burn *lightning* grooves down the length of the shaft. These have been called "blood grooves," but do not serve this purpose. I believe these grooves help to keep the arrow straight and they may make good *spirit*.

It is time for the easy work. Get feathers, lots of feathers, and sort them into piles of *lefts* (those that turn to the left) and *rights*. Feathers from any bird will work and primary feathers are the best. My personal preference is to use goose, duck or wild turkey feathers. Remember when gathering feathers that the eagle, hawk, owl, falcon and other raptors are protected by federal law.

Useable feathers are like a good shaft, they must be strong and stiff. Tail feathers are usually not stiff enough and this is important as the fletching takes a good deal of abuse both in the quiver and going across the hand.

Now for the part that requires skill. Choose a feather from the two piles (lefts and rights) and place the large end in a vise. Hold the feather by the other end (top) firmly. Grasp the outer side of the feather with your free hand and slowly pull out, down and back with constant pressure and speed. This is called *stripping*. If the vane hangs up at any point, then move your grip further down the vane. If the vane sticks and you continue to pull without moving your grip, you will tear the vane. This method will yield two vanes per feather if you are careful. Never place two vanes from the same feather on a shaft as it will not fly right. The same goes for putting a right and a left feather on the same shaft; the arrow will try to fly left and right at the same time.

CHEYENNE   SHOSHONI   MODOC/ YUROK

KIOWA/ OSAGE   BLACKFOOT   MANDAN

LAKOTAH   LAKOTAH   LAKOTAH

ILLUSTRATION OF NOCK FOUND ON OLD INDIAN ARROWS

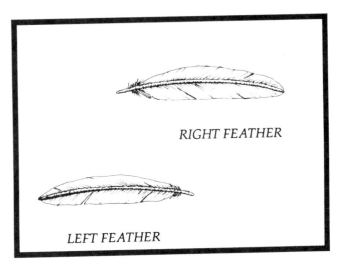

RIGHT FEATHER

LEFT FEATHER

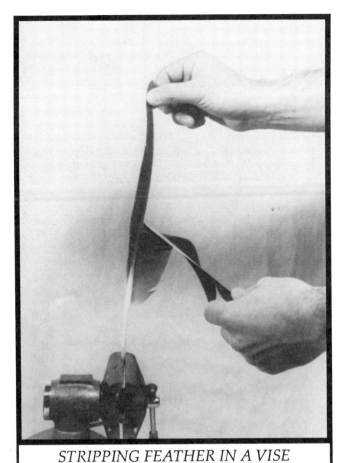

STRIPPING FEATHER IN A VISE

this makes them easier to work with, and they will lie closer to the shaft. Now place one end of the shaft under one arm while holding the nock end in the same hand and place the vane on the shaft and lash one turn around the shaft and over the tail of the vane. Make sure that you place the first fletching on the shaft at a right angle to the nock or the arrow will not leave the bow properly. Now lash the other two vanes equidistant from each other and from the first vane.

Some craftspersons like to trim the vanes at this point. I do not. It seems that once the vane is stable, glued and tied, the cut is easier to make and will be more consistent. Decide for yourself which technique works best.

The Indian arrows I have worked with all have straight fletchings. Most of the fletchings are quite long being five to seven inches in length. You may wish to add a touch of spiral or helix to the vanes as this helps to stabilize the arrow faster after it comes off the bow. It also makes the arrow fly a bit more smoothly. If you do spiral the vane, the side of that feather that would have faced downward on the bird is the side that should face into the wind on the shaft.

Once you have decided how you want the feathers to lie, you need to tie down the other end of the fletching. Pull the first vane down and lash it tight. Some arrow makers (including the author) like to glue down the entire feather length before lashing down the front. Hide glue is best for this, but barge cement will work just fine. Now glue and/or tie down the other two vanes in the same manner. Make sure you cover the ends of the front tails.

Now glue the lashing at the front and back of the fletching. If you use real sinew on the vanes, rub hide glue over the lashing. Use any type of clear glue on artificial sinew or linen lashing as hide glue will not work with artificial lashings.

There is an alternative to this method of attaching vanes. Indians of South America, as well as some of the North American Natives, lashed on the vanes in reverse and then folded them over

Incidentally, there is an alternative to stripping. You can split a feather using a razor blade and then sand or grind the pitch off the vane but the vane will not lay as close to the shaft and stripped vanes last much longer. Practice stripping on old junky feathers. A good hint to more successful stripping is to steam the feathers straight before attempting to strip them.

Sort the stripped feathers according to length, width and height. Place them in groups of three. Cut the groups of three to equal length but do not worry about height until later. Cut small tails in each end of the vane; these will be used for lashing the vanes to the shaft.

A number of different materials can be used to lash down the vanes. Sinew (either real or artificial), dental floss, or waxed linen all work well. If artificial sinew or waxed linen is used, then it will need to be split.

Put your vanes in water to soak overnight as

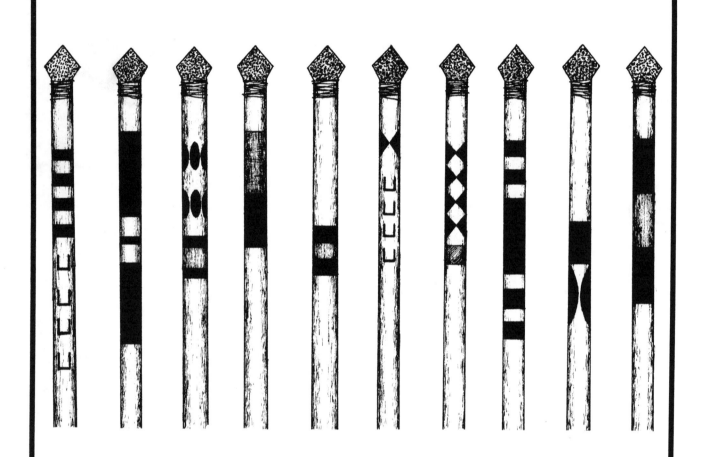

ACTUAL ARROW CRESTS FOUND ON INDIAN ARROWS

so that there is no lashing at the nock point. Many contend that this is easier.

Based on what they have seen in museums and reference books, some arrow makers do not glue the entire length of the fletching to the shaft. What they fail to take into account, however, is that these arrows are over a hundred years old and that the glues on them were not impervious to heat or moisture. Most of these arrows were found on battlefields or in private collections which too often do not receive proper care. This is why the fletchings are very rarely found still properly glued; most museum curators will explain this with a higher degree of articulation than is written here. This is another good point to research on your own.

Since your feathers were wet when placed on the shaft, you will need to steam them over (not in) a pot of boiling water. Simply hold them over the steam for a short period of time and they'll go back to their natural state. Once the vane is back to normal, it needs to be trimmed. Most vanes on Indian arrows measure from 1/32" to 1/8" in height in the front and from 1/4" to 1/2" at the back. To begin, trim them a bit high as you can always cut them down. If the vanes are too high, they will whistle in flight and will not fly far. You do not have to worry about them being too low. Historical research shows fletchings were quite high until around 1650. About that time, someone realized the function of the fletching is to keep the back of the shaft from passing the front of the shaft, and that it doesn't take much of a feather to act as a good rudder. Considering the bow arrived on the Plains only some 2000 years ago, this is quite an evolution. Arrows were originally fletched tangentially (the entire feather was

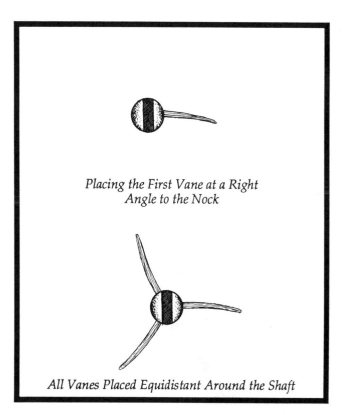

Placing the First Vane at a Right Angle to the Nock

All Vanes Placed Equidistant Around the Shaft

tied to the shaft in a flat form) instead of the radial fletching used today. This shows the keen engineering the Indian developed in a relatively short period of time. At present, fletch your arrows with a long, thin feather and they will be historically correct as well as faster in flight.

Once the vane is trimmed, the arrow is nearly complete and should be tested. Get your bow and some hay bales; soft dirt or a sand hill will also work. Shoot the arrows repeatedly and find those few arrows that shoot better than the others. Mark them well with paint or marks of some kind. Store these arrows standing up, not in a quiver and grease them every year or so and they will always shoot well. They may be used for hunting, competition or simply to

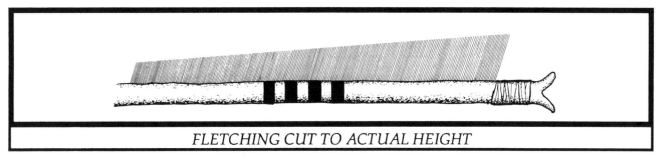

FLETCHING CUT TO ACTUAL HEIGHT

SEVENTEEN STEPS TO MAKING ARROWS

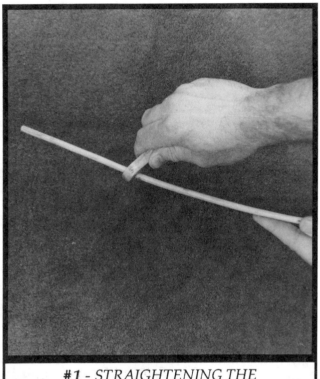

#1 - STRAIGHTENING THE ARROW SHAFT

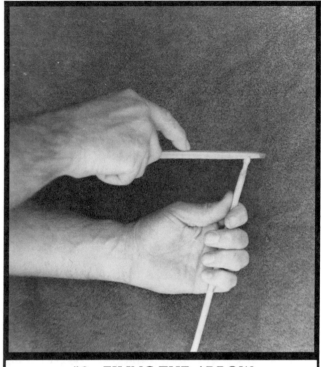

#2 - FILING THE ARROW NOCK

#3 - COMPLETED SHAFT
(Notice the Enlarged Nock)

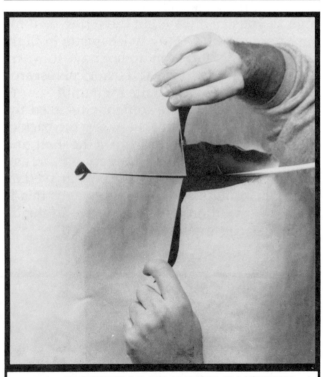

#4 - STRIPPING FEATHER IN TEETH
(Both Sides of the Feather at Once)

#5 - VANES READY FOR SHAFT

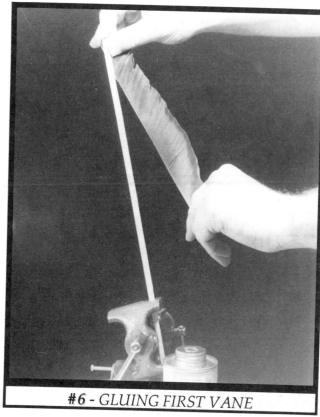

#6 - GLUING FIRST VANE

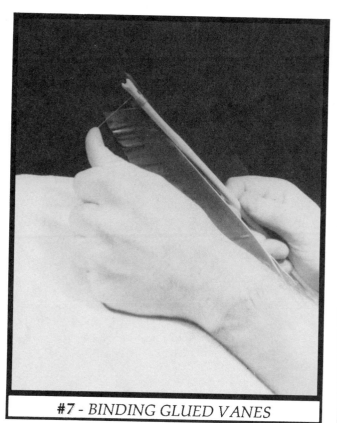

#7 - BINDING GLUED VANES

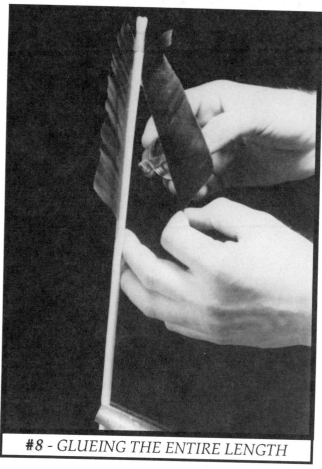

#8 - GLUEING THE ENTIRE LENGTH

#9 - PULL UP TO LET GLUE GET TACKY

#10 - BINDING FRONT TAIL OF VANES

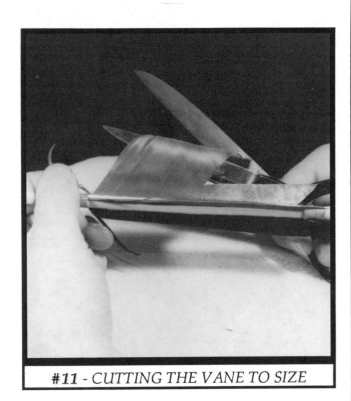

#11 - CUTTING THE VANE TO SIZE

#12 - TOOLS FOR POUNDING ARROW HEADS

66

#13 - *POUNDED NAIL ARROW HEAD*

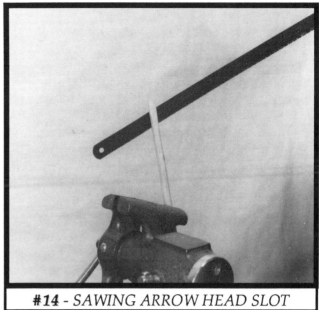

#14 - *SAWING ARROW HEAD SLOT*

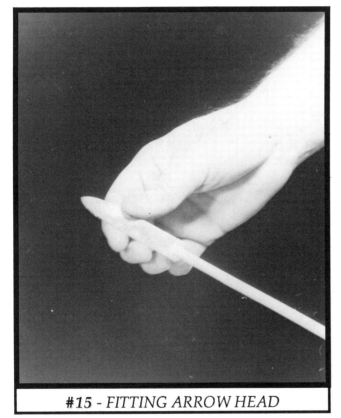

#15 - *FITTING ARROW HEAD*

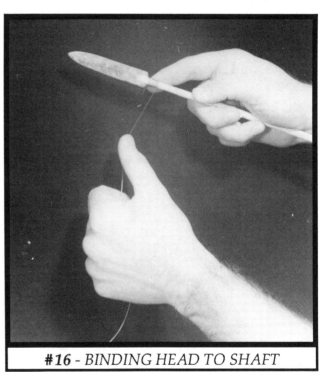

#16 - *BINDING HEAD TO SHAFT*

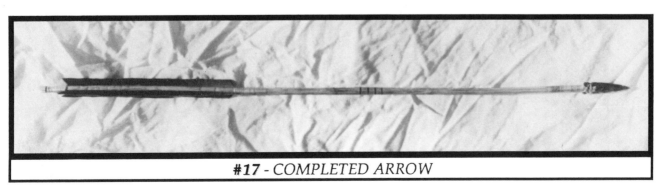

#17 - *COMPLETED ARROW*

impress your friends.

✠ ✠ ✠

Many historians have proclaimed that the placement of the arrowhead was determined by whether the arrow was to be used for war or for hunting. If the arrowhead was horizontal to the ground when released from the bow, they reason that, as a man's ribs are in a horizontal position, the arrow was made for war. Using the same logic, if the head was vertical the arrow was meant for hunting animals as their ribs run in that direction. After examining hundreds of arrows in private collections and museums, I doubt very much that this is true. Arrow makers both old and new are well aware that even the straightest of fletchings will not keep an arrow from spinning as it leaves the bow, making head placement a moot point.

Generally, there are five materials which are used to make arrowheads: Bone, antler, stone, wood and steel. If you have access to, or can make, some stone points, you are that much ahead. Stone is good for hunting (though ille-gal in most states), but will not work for target shooting. The art of knapping, however, is a subject to be delved into on another day.

Wood is only useable when you have the means to make an end that is rounded or blunt. I have seen wooden marbles glued to a shaft and this makes an excellent arrow for small game and birds. A clean hit with a *wood blunt* is preferable, especially on a skunk, to a bad hit with steel. At times you can find wood with a natural mutation that makes a good blunt. Wild rose is great for this. By the way, leave the vanes on a bird arrow a bit longer than those on target or flight arrows. If, by some rare chance, you miss the shot, the arrow won't go as far with higher vanes.

Bone is great for hunting but, like stone, cannot be used for target practice. Using a hacksaw and a file, you can make razor sharp points on bone. This material also looks good and is very authentic. Another natural material that pro-vides a workable alternative is antler. Antler can be shot into bales of hay for target practice, but an antler won't take the edge that bone will.

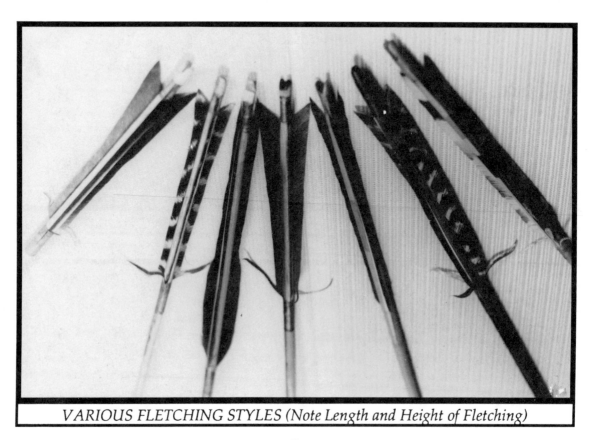

VARIOUS FLETCHING STYLES (Note Length and Height of Fletching)

Last, but not least, is metal. Barrel hoops, old horseshoe nails pounded flat, files, etc. all make great metal heads. Some of the banding steels used today are made of a carbide that holds a great edge. If you can locate an old-time blacksmith, he can fashion heads out of almost anything but be wary of metals with a lot of shine. Bright metal arrowheads look cheap and can possibly scare away game.

☩ ☩ ☩

Remember all of those Hollywood movies where the Indians shot flaming arrows into wagons? Most of that is Hollywood, but Indians did occasionally burn wagons and, as a by-product, think of all of the knives, lances and arrowheads they could make from the wagon rims and tongue hitches!

When the arrowheads are complete, they need to be placed on the shaft. Using a hacksaw or scroll saw, cut a straight slot in the shaft. Place the head in the shaft and see how it fits. If you are using stone or bone heads, you may have to

ARROW HEAD STYLES

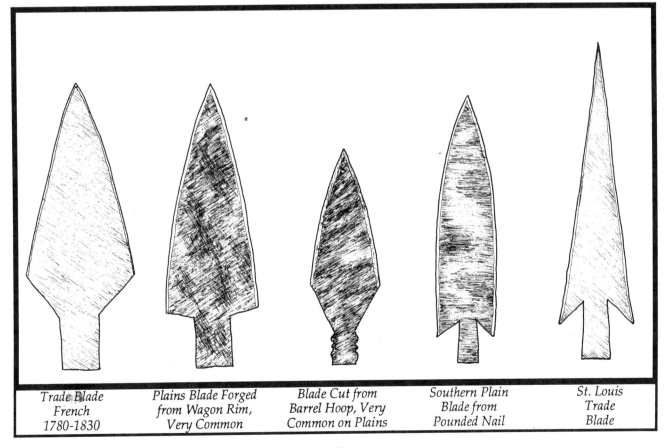

| *Trade Blade French 1780-1830* | *Plains Blade Forged from Wagon Rim, Very Common* | *Blade Cut from Barrel Hoop, Very Common on Plains* | *Southern Plain Blade from Pounded Nail* | *St. Louis Trade Blade* |

69

cut a larger slot than is needed for steel. Once you have a good firm fit, take the head out of the slot and sand the end of the shaft at an angle so that the shaft tapers into a smooth extension of the head. Place the head back into the slot and glue it in place with hide glue, pine pitch, epoxy or barge cement. Let this dry for awhile and then lash the head to the shaft with the same material used for the fletching. Once this is accomplished, let the arrow dry in an upright position. As soon as it is dry, and if you have been patient and careful, you should be proud of your new arrow. Make some for your friends and - happy shooting!

HEADS MADE OF NAIL, BONE, STONE, STEEL AND WOOD BLUNT

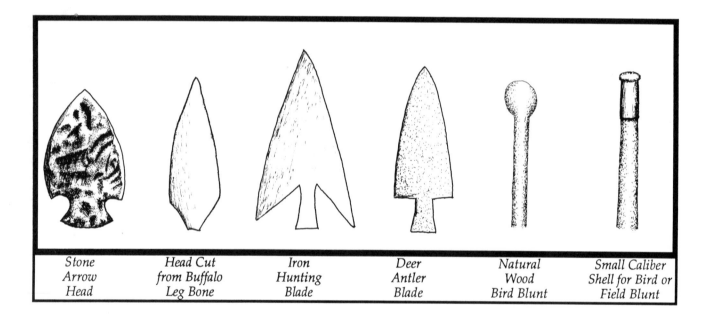

| Stone Arrow Head | Head Cut from Buffalo Leg Bone | Iron Hunting Blade | Deer Antler Blade | Natural Wood Bird Blunt | Small Caliber Shell for Bird or Field Blunt |

CASES AND QUIVERS

Although a quiver is not an essential piece of archery tackle, it is difficult to examine primitive bows and arrows without seeing them. Most collections have a quiver or case for every bow and arrow set. Actually, the quiver is usually thought of when referring to the Woodlands tribes. The Plains tribes used a combination bow case and quiver arrangement. The length of the bows used by the Woodland tribes did not permit passage between trees in the forest if the bow were strapped on their backs. Many movies portray the Indian with a bow strapped across his back with the bow braced. Most historians do not agree with this portrayal as it is not good for the limbs to leave the bow braced for long periods of time unless it is being fired. Further, the bow is less accessible when carried in this manner.

Most of the California and Southwestern tribes used one case to hold both bow and arrows. In fact, many of the Southwestern cases had a slot inside the quiver to carry an extra bow.

The Plains-type bow case and quiver is a different breed of carrying gear because of the way it is made. It usually consists of a very long strap, to which a short skin tube, large enough to hold thirty to forty arrows, is tied. Over or under the short tube is a long tube that is capable of holding a bow, or sometimes two. The Plains bow cases and quivers are made out of nearly every kind of animal hide possible. Buffalo, elk, goat, cougar, otter, buckskin and rabbit have all been observed as materials for bow cases and quivers. The Nez Perce and the Crow are particularly well known for their highly decorated otter case and quiver combinations of the late 1800s. These were usually profusely beaded and hung with tassels. The Lakotah people made most of their cases and quivers out of otter and mountain lion. Most often, the hair was left on the skin and this was on the

outside of the case. A few have been observed with the hair on the inside of the bow case, but this was generally done by the Southwestern tribes. The hair not only looks good, it also serves as a noise dampener and keeps moisture away from the bow. This is very important when the bow is backed with sinew.

✠ ✠ ✠

Cases made from the hide of a mountain lion have the tail and the feet left intact as dangles. Beaded and quilled pendants were added to the openings of the tubes to complete the ensemble. The legs of the lion serve to make the

NEZ PERCE/CROW-STYLE MOUNTAIN LION BOWCASE AND QUIVER MADE BY GEORGE KNOWLDEN

71

strap that holds the affair on the back. You can easily get a case and quiver out of an average size lion hide.

✠ ✠ ✠

To make a quiver of otter, it will take three otter skins of average size, or two very large skins. Depending on the length of the bow, the bow case uses a cut down otter skin, while the quiver uses a full skin. Since the bow case is very narrow, strips are cut out of the belly to form the straps for the set. The tails are usually cut off the skin and beaded or quilled. The decorated tails are then sewn back on the openings of the tubes to form pendants. The scrap strips of skin are cut into pieces one-half inch wide and bunched together. Two bunches of strips are used as tassels hanging from the bottom of the quiver. A rawhide disc is sewn into the end of the quiver, and covered with grass and cedar bark. This holds the arrowheads apart in the quiver and keeps them from sliding out the end.

Cases and quivers made of skunk and bobcat have been observed as well, particularly among the Cheyenne, Blackfoot and Plateau tribes. It takes three or four skunks to make an outfit, and two average size bobcats. One skunk skin bow case and quiver recently examined had a rawhide tube inside of the fur case. This idea is especially useful when working with thin-skinned animals as after a few years of use, the skins of the smaller animals seem to deteriorate and fall apart. With the heavy use that a bow case and quiver get, this would certainly be a problem. The rawhide tube inside the fur would eliminate some of the wear and tear on the skin.

✠ ✠ ✠

A friend recently asked, "Why not use a beaver for the bow case and quiver?" Only a buckskinner true to heart would ask this question. These days it would be no problem to get beaver and no one could say it was not historically correct. However, as far as I know, there are not any

SKUNK BOWCASE AND QUIVER,
CHEYENNE-STYLE, MADE BY
C. RINDLISBACHER OF RED HAWK TRADING
(Note the Rawhide Support)

CLOSE-UP OF THE SKUNK BOWCASE AND QUIVER MADE BY C. RINDLISBACHER

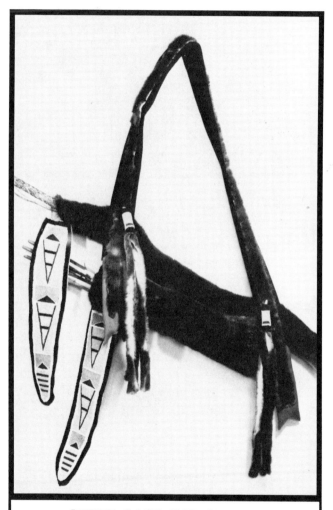

OTTER CASE AND QUIVER MADE IN THE CROW FASHION BY TERRY ROSENLUND

bow cases and quivers in any museum or collection that are fashioned from beaver hide. It is probable that the Indian did not use beaver pelts for economic reasons. The Indians used beaver hides or *plews* for trade and were thereby able to acquire beads, cloth, metal and even guns. If a beaver hide was worth more in beads than it would be worth as a bow case, or better yet, if it could be traded for beads for a bow case, why not use a more available and less profitable hide for the case and quiver? By the time the mountain men were no longer trading, most of the beaver were gone. Other skins were more plentiful and better looking. This, in my opinion, is why no beaver skin bow cases or quivers are found in museums today.

✠ ✠ ✠

Bow cases usually cover all but four or five inches of the bow. If the bottom or top of the bow has a hair pendant attached, this is the end that hangs out of the bow case. The length of the quiver has long been a point of debate. Many of the quivers in museums hold either

73

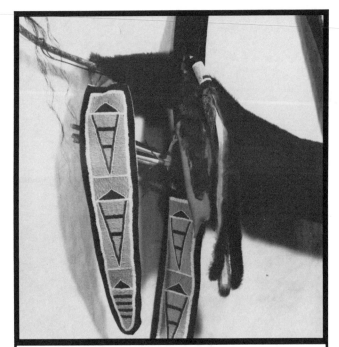

*CLOSE-UP OF THE OTTER CASE
AND QUIVER MADE BY
TERRY ROSENLUND*

In addition to being attractive, cases and quivers have a number of functions. Many times the case was used as a day pack during a hunt. Extra strings, dry hide glue, extra sinew strands, *was'na* (a form of pemmican), spare arrow heads, and flint and steel could all be attached to the strap or stored in the case. The cedar bark placed at the bottom of the quiver to separate the arrow heads was often used for fire tinder. This bark also served to keep the arrow heads quiet in the quiver. A spare bow could be tied beneath the case or the quiver. Extra arrow shafts have been found tied to the quiver in order to keep it straight and open while in use. Many of the quivers observed have only a stick or rawhide to keep them straight. Bow cases rarely have a stick to keep them straight as they do not really require one.

✠ ✠ ✠

Understanding that the case and quiver are both beautiful and practical is not enough. It is true that case and quiver decoration, today as in the past, are a social statement. This tackle was also used as a carrying bag for short trips, but knowing this does not fully account for the uses and functions of the case and quiver.

The English wear the quiver on the right hip or

the entire arrow (to the nock) or half of the arrow is exposed. The paintings of Catlin, Bodmer and Wissler, lead one to believe that the quivers held only the bare shaft. Little of the fletching, if any, is inside the quiver opening. This makes sense because on a running horse or even on a walking warrior, the quiver would damage the fletchings.

✠ ✠ ✠

This suggests that many museums are incorrect in their arrow/quiver displays. This is not surprising. I recall once telling a conservator that the sinew side of a bow (which had been strung backwards) was the back, not the belly of the bow. I was told that I was not qualified in such matters and dismissed, yet this was the conservator of a very well-known museum of Indian art. In any event, I would suggest that Catlin, Laubin and Hamilton are correct. The fletchings should extend beyond the opening of the quiver to preserve the feathers.

✠ ✠ ✠

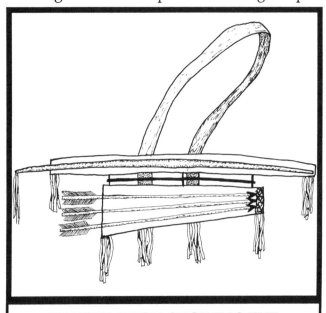

*ILLUSTRATION SHOWING THE
METHOD IN WHICH BOW AND ARROWS
ARE CARRIED IN CASE & QUIVER*

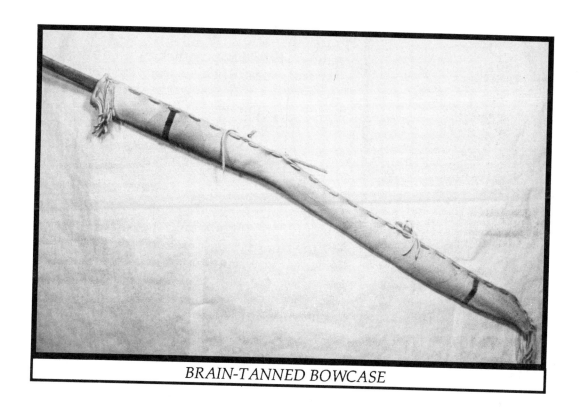

BRAIN-TANNED BOWCASE

BRAIN-TANNED BOWCASE
WITH ADDED STRAP

shoulder as they shoot, making the right hand grasp the arrow in an awkward, dramatic manner. Errol Flynn somehow made this look easy and graceful in his *Robin Hood* movies, but I dare say that most archers are not actors. Even the left shoulder would have been more natural for the right-handed bowman.

⊞ ⊞ ⊞

The hip quiver is the type used by most modern archers as it is easily accessed. Some even wear the quiver on their left hip instead of the right. For the right-handed archer, this is a lot more sensible. Lowering the bow, reaching behind the string, grasping the arrow and then reversing the whole process just to nock the arrow is rather silly. With the quiver on the left hip, you simply reach over the waist and grasp the arrow. As the arrow hand goes to its natural place on the string, the arrow follows suit.

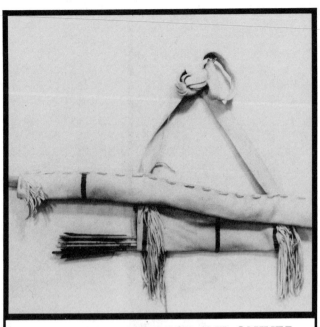

BRAIN-TANNED CASE AND QUIVER IN A COMPLETE OUTFIT

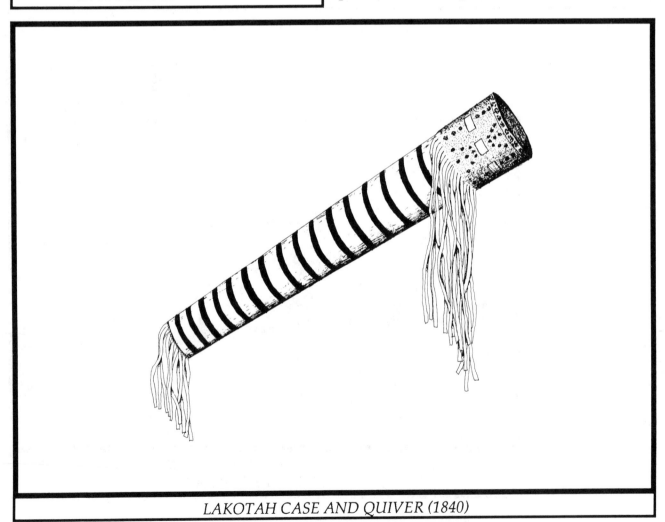

LAKOTAH CASE AND QUIVER (1840)

This is why the Indian wore his quiver on the left side of his body if he was right-handed. The case of arrows did not usually go as low as the waist, but rather hung under the armpit or perhaps slightly lower. Most bow cases and quiver combinations found in museums today indicate that the set was to be worn on the left. Old movies (*e.g.*, "Buffalo Bill"), paintings, and photos (Curtis), all show the quiver under the left armpit. Either most Indians were left-handed or these examples are incorrect. Both Laubin and Hamilton write that the quiver was either worn on the left or tied across the lap while running buffalo. This would keep the quiver from bouncing and help prevent losing the arrows.

✠ ✠ ✠

Unfortunately, most museums would not permit photos of their cases and quivers to be published. The examples in this book are either from my personal collection or belong to fellow archers. There are many photos in museum catalogues and reference books. Find what pleases you and is complimentary to the bow you have made, and then create it.

*SHOOTING INDIAN STYLE
NOTICE THE CONVENIENT QUIVER
POSITION ON THE LEFT SIDE*

*UNFINISHED BOWCASE AND QUIVER
MADE OF OTTER SKIN (LAKOTAH)*

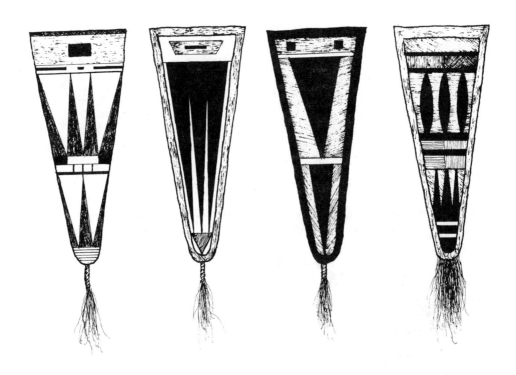

QUIVER PENDANTS FOUND ON CROW/NEZ PERCE CASES AND QUIVERS

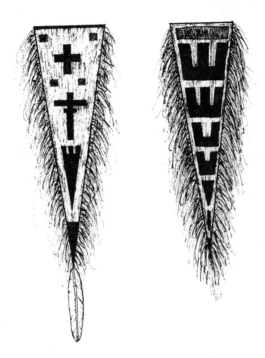

PENDANTS FOUND ON LAKOTAH CASES AND QUIVERS

SHOOTING INDIAN STYLE

"Just how accurate is the primitive bow?" This question is asked by nearly every non-primitive archer that sees a traditional bow. Most of them raise their eyebrows when I recount Hansard's story (1841:25) of Indians firing their arrows into the air at an upward angle and pinning birds to the ground at a distance of one hundred yards. Dr. James Howard (1947) related the story of Lakotah Indians hitting a charcoal spot the size of a silver dollar while at a full run on horseback. Many seem to dismiss these stories as "historical exaggerations." Still, many people were present when Beth Denner, of Utah, repeatedly shot an apple at a distance of thirty yards. Even more were present at the Primitive Nationals when I placed three arrows into a paper plate at a distance of two hundred, twenty-five yards. This may have been luck, but that isn't likely. The bow can only be as accurate as the archer shooting it and the more familiar the archer is with the bow, the better. This chapter discusses some shooting methods, release techniques and historically correct shooting styles.

✠ ✠ ✠

Before release, posture, etc., can be examined the bow and arrow placement need to be properly matched. The point of arrow placement on the string is called the *nocking point*. On a modern bow this is marked with a small brass ring known as a nock set. You can use a nock set on your string, but it will not be primitive. Some archers tie a knot of leather on the string or mark the string with a piece of charcoal or magic marker. Historical evidence shows that primitive shooters did not mark the string.

To determine the proper nocking point you will need some hay bales or a sandy bank, three or four unfletched arrows, the bow, and something to mark the string. Hold the bow so that it is comfortable. This will become your permanent hold, so you may wish to experiment with different positions on the handle. Nock an unfletched arrow and allow it to rest on the top of the bow hand. *Cant*, or angle, the bow at a forty-five (45°) degree angle. This helps the arrow to stay on your hand during the draw. It will also help compensate for the string not being flush. Stand about six feet back from the sand hill or bales. Draw back one of the unfletched arrows. Although many release techniques will be discussed later in this chapter, for now use the one with which you are most familiar. Shoot the arrow. If it goes into the target "nock up," then you need to lower the nocking point on the string. If it goes into the target with the "nock low," you will need to lower the point where the arrow fits the string. Shoot another unfletched arrow from the new nocking point and check how it strikes the target. The whole idea behind this exercise is to get the arrow to strike the target in a straight line. You may have to shoot a dozen arrows or more to get the correct point but when you do, mark the string well. Start this exercise by shooting the arrow at nearly ninety (90°) degrees; this should save you some time.

✠ ✠ ✠

With the nocking point established and the hand gripping the bow properly, how should you stand when you shoot? This is where many primitive archers run into trouble. They have learned the position adopted by Her Majesty's Archers where the feet are perpendicular to the target, the bow arm is fully extended, the string is drawn to the cheek (tightly anchored) and firing is done using the Mediterranean release. Consistency is the first and foremost key to accuracy in shooting and this method works just fine with a full drawn arrow and a longbow. But a short bow with its short

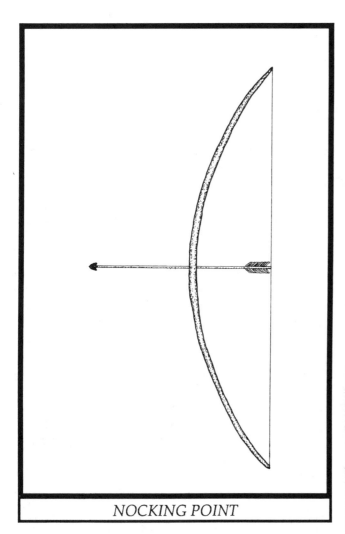

NOCKING POINT

general, the Plains draw was bow above head, drawing the arrow as it was brought down to bear on the target. The arrow was released as soon as the head reaches the bow hand.

✠ ✠ ✠

From which side of the bow should you shoot? This depends, of course, on whether you are right or left-handed. Traditionally the left-handed archer released from the right side of the bow and the right-handed archer released from the left. Thomas Mails, a respected historian of Indian ways, claims that most warriors released from the right side of the bow, but most other authorities on Indian archery dispute this. Hamilton, Laubin, Schuyler, Powell, Wooden Leg and Pope have all stated that most Plains and California archers released from the

PROPER STANCE FOR INDIAN STYLE SHOOTING

arrows cannot be drawn fist to eye as the limbs will over stress. So, how do you shoot?

The Indian way requires that the draw, aim and release be done in one motion, making a firm and positive anchor point impossible. Stand with your feet towards, but angled slightly to the right or left of the target. Hold the bow arm nearly extended with the bow canted to the right if the arrow is on the left, and to the left if the arrow is on the right of the bow. In this kind of archery, there is no set anchor point as shooting conditions may vary. Having the top of the hand locked at the chin or the wrist against the breast are good anchoring methods.

As you draw the string and arrow back with the arrow hand, push out with the bow hand, making this one smooth motion; this is very similar to the breast stroke in swimming. In

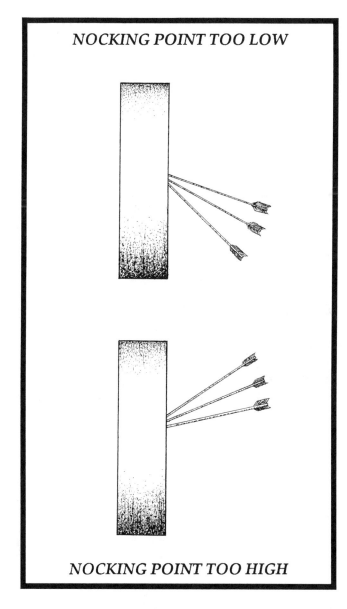

NOCKING POINT TOO LOW

NOCKING POINT TOO HIGH

blunts by his grandfather or uncles. He learned to shoot while lying down, standing up, from a horse, under a robe, in a tree, or at a full run going backwards or forwards. The targets used for practice were always small, such as an upright arrow, a clod of dirt or a moccasin thrown in the air. Most archers today can only hope to be so accurate in any of these postures. But it also needs to be kept in mind that the bow was the main means by which the home was protected and food procured.

✠ ✠ ✠

The release is another very important key to being accurate. A solid, clean release will make the difference between a hit and a miss. Most of us grew up using a technique called the *primary release.* It is a very natural hold and is solid and clean. The only problem is that it cannot be easily used with a bow of twenty pounds or more at full draw. This is the release used by most Indian kids while growing up.

As white kids grow up and go to Scout camp they are taught to forget the natural primary grip and learn the more sophisticated English (also called Mediterranean) release. This is the three finger anchored grip that has been around for centuries in Europe. This is also where the Indian's archery begins to differ from all other types.

As Indian children grew older and built stronger bows, the primary grip that was so

left side of the bow. This would only seem fitting as most artists have drawn Indians shooting with their quivers under their left armpit. If, however, the thumb release was used, the arrow was most likely fired off the right side of the bow. Different releases and their merits are discussed in more detail below.

✠ ✠ ✠

Earlier I wrote that consistency is the major key to accuracy. This is true even though the above method may not sound very consistent. The only thing consistent about the way an Indian shot was his accuracy. From the moment a boy could walk he was given a bow and arrow

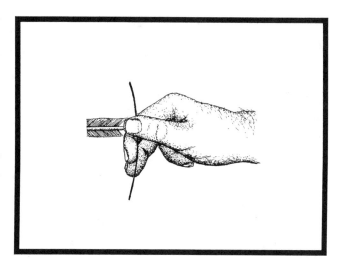

#1 - PROPER USE OF THE QUIVER

#2 - THE DRAW

#3 - THE AIM

#4 - RELEASE AND FOLLOW THROUGH

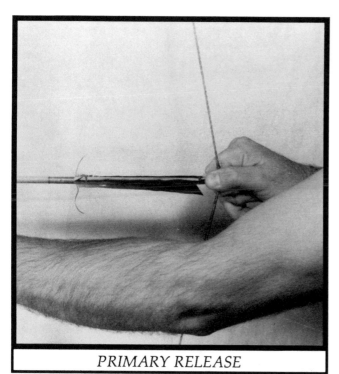

PRIMARY RELEASE

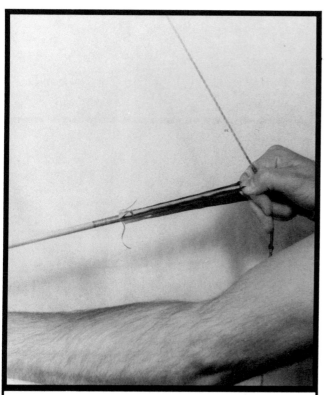

SECONDARY OR AUGMENTED RELEASE

familiar was not discarded; they simply augmented the release by placing the middle and ring fingers on the string. This is called the *augmented* or *secondary* release. It appears to be the most prevalent method of release used on both the Plains and in California. The other dominant form of release is called the *tertiary* release. This is still an augmented primary release, but unlike the secondary release, it uses only the index and middle fingers for support as the ring finger is folded back into the palm. The tertiary is not my choice of release as it leaves the fingers sore and chafed after a long shooting session. If you grew up with this release, however, you would probably develop callouses on your fingers.

✠ ✠ ✠

Another type of release that may have been used by the Plains Indians is one that only the Orientals and Turks have been known to use. This release allows the thumb to come around and hold the string with a device known as a *thumb ring*. The only reference to this is a painting by Remington titled *Last Herd* where the archer pictured appears to be using a thumb release. Some artifacts thought to be thumb rings have been found in archaeological digs in the south, but there is no proof that the Plains Indians ever used this release. Ishi was observed using the thumb or Mongolian release without a thumb ring, but to quote Pope, "Few Nations use this release, and the Yana (Ishi's tribe) appear to be the only American Natives to do so." All this neither proves nor disproves the case, but knowing and understanding Plains and California Indian archery leads me to believe that they did not use a thumb release.

✠ ✠ ✠

An often asked question is why the Eskimo used the Mediterranean release and the Plains people did not. This brings to mind some interesting concepts. First, the Eskimo had contact with Asian people who did use the Mediterranean release. We know this relationship existed as evidenced by similarities in culture, religion, physical features and bows.

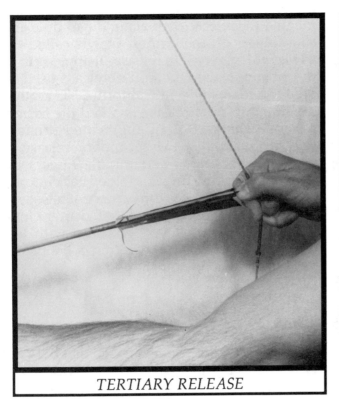

TERTIARY RELEASE

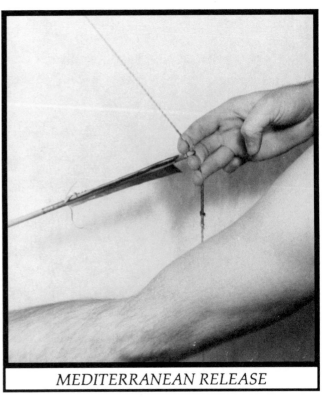

MEDITERRANEAN RELEASE

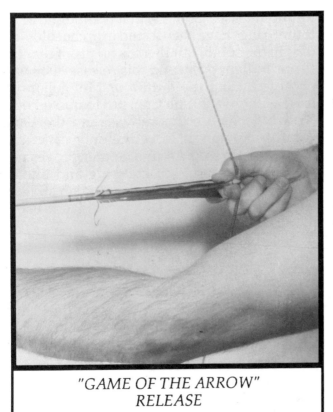

"GAME OF THE ARROW"
RELEASE

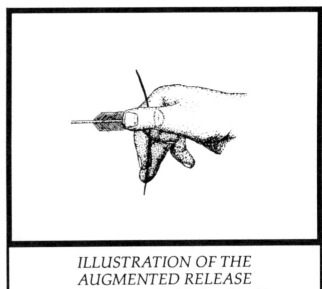

ILLUSTRATION OF THE
AUGMENTED RELEASE
(Notice the Lack of String Pinch)

Second, the Plains and California peoples did not use the Mediterranean release because the style was so alien from the primary release. The Plains bows are very short and this will cause a great deal of finger pinch at the index finger when the arrow reaches full draw. Third, the secondary release allows the arrow to be nocked and drawn in one motion. The Eskimo, with his longer bow and lack of the horse, was not concerned with shooting quickly. Therefore, he could use the slower and better anchored Mediterranean release.

There is one last type of release which was used by the Lakotah Sioux, Cheyenne and, perhaps, some other tribes. There are no references to its existence in written or painted form and I have only seen it as shown in Buffalo Bill movies exhibited at the Cody Museum in Cody, Wyoming. I have, however, spoken with the grandsons of warriors and they have verified that this release existed and was used at one point in time. The release has no name but I have labeled it the *game of the arrow* release. With this release even the most practiced archer will

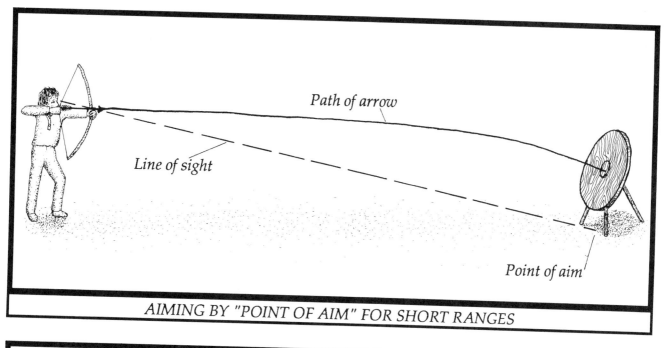

AIMING BY "POINT OF AIM" FOR SHORT RANGES

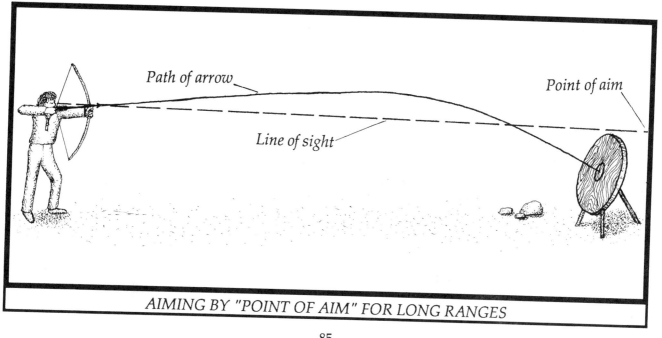

AIMING BY "POINT OF AIM" FOR LONG RANGES

85

sacrifice accuracy, but the speed with which an arrow may be nocked and released is remarkable. Accuracy, of course, becomes a relative term in that a good shooter, with this release, could place a dozen arrows into an area the size of a horse at thirty yards in less than fifteen seconds. In battle, this release would have been very handy at either close distances or far range when raining arrows on the enemy. This is also the release I believe the Indians used while shooting arrows into the air. The object of the game is to see how many arrows you can get into the air before the first arrow hits the ground, hence the name *game of the arrow*. Catlin claimed that Mandan and Lakotah warriors could get eight or nine arrows into the air at once. Using this release I can get five and almost six in the air at one time. With a standard release, I can barely get three up at once.

✠ ✠ ✠

This is the technique: Keep in mind that most warriors carried five or six arrows in the bow hand in addition to those in his quiver. It works best for me when the nocks of the arrows are pointing up and to the right. Nock the first arrow by holding it between your thumb and forefinger on the <u>outside</u> of the bow string. With this method of shooting, the arrow comes off the right side of the grip instead of the left. Quickly reach <u>around</u> the bow string and grasp the next arrow firmly, nock and fire. Continue to shoot this way until all of the arrows are gone. By the way, if you are practicing the *game of arrows* by shooting into the air, don't shoot straight up or your friends may begin calling you "arrowhead."

✠ ✠ ✠

After you are able to stand comfortably and you have your release chosen and practiced, how do you hit the target? There are basically two methods of aiming. One is called the *point of aim* method and the other is called instinctive aiming. Point of aim is a type of shooting where you line up the head of the arrow with something of relative height to the target. What you need to do is find a spot on the ground for short ranges (forty yards or less) or a mark that is higher than the target for long distances (those

ANCHORING FROM THE CHIN

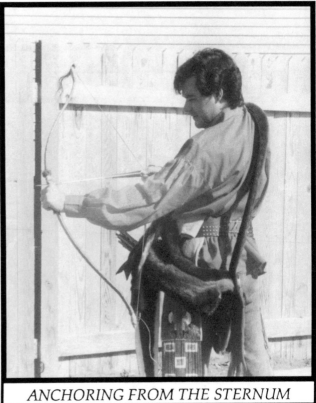

ANCHORING FROM THE STERNUM

86

ANCHORING ACROSS THE CHEST

PROPER POSITION OF QUIVER & CASE

over fifty yards) that the head of the arrow can be visually rested upon.

If you always line up the head of the arrow on this marker, your arrow will fly and land in the same place every time. For example, if you wish to find the point of aim at a distance of forty yards, using a forty-eight inch bow with a forty pound draw weight, and twenty-three inch arrows, the mark or point will be about halfway between you and the target. Draw the arrow so that you can sight diagonally down the head of the arrow. Follow this imaginary line to the ground and then place a marker (a rock or cow chip will be fine) where your eye rests. Draw the arrow and visually rest the arrowhead on this marker; release the arrow. If your shot goes beyond the target, move the marker closer to you. If the arrow falls short of the target, move the marker farther away. Right or left deficiencies can be dealt with by moving the marker for correction. It is very important when using the point of aim method that you constantly fix your eye on the marker. You see the target only in the back of your

mind, if at all. Practice often and you will quickly understand and master this method of shooting.

✠ ✠ ✠

Instinctive shooting is exactly what the name implies. You simply see the arrow striking the target before you shoot. All Indian archery I know of has been the instinctive type. When running a horse at a buffalo or shooting at an enemy that is shooting at you, there is little time to find the point of aim to mark the deadly shot.

The only way to learn to shoot instinctively is to practice shooting under a variety of circumstances. Play golf using a bow and arrow. Go into an empty field and shoot with your eyes closed or with a blindfold. Just remember to keep facing in the direction the arrow was pointed after the shot so that you don't lose the arrows. Some say the instinctive shooter is not as accurate but I think the opposite is true. Howard Hill was an instinctive shooter and we have all seen the movie *Robin Hood* where he split arrows with arrows for Errol Flynn. That's hard to do at three yards. Try it at twenty-five.

✠ ✠ ✠

Should you desire to hunt with a primitive bow, in addition to target shooting, it will help if you can learn the instinctive aiming method. Birds on the wing and animals on the run simply will not hold still while the shot is aligned and there is rarely a tree or fence post to use as a marker when you need one.

As noted before, this method is not necessarily better than others, it just happens to be the way I shoot. I have an aversion to modern sights and their lack of convenience. The instinctive method, coupled with a familiar shot, makes for a deadly combination. It is also very traditional.

✠ ✠ ✠

Still not hitting the target? This bring us to an important point of archery. In previous chapters it was mentioned that the string on the primitive bow does not allow the arrow to rest flush with the center of the bow. If the spine of the arrow is not properly matched to the bow, the arrow will never fly straight. It works like this: When the arrow is drawn back and released, the bow string has a constant tendency to return to the center of the bow. This creates an angle that, in theory, will throw the arrow to the left or right depending on from which side of the bow the arrow is released. Either way, the string desires the center of the bow and this is referred to as the *Archer's Paradox*. The resolution of this paradox is to be sure that the arrows are spined correctly for the weight of the bow. This does not mean the arrow should weigh a specific amount, but that it should bend a certain amount near the middle of the arrow. Let's look at what happens when the arrow is not spined correctly. If the arrow has too much give or bend in the center, then the angle of the returning string will cause the arrow to bend around the handle too much. This will cause the arrow to fly to the right of the target (assuming that the arrow is released from the left side of the bow). It will also cause

the fletching to strike the handle of the bow. If the flex or bend of the arrow is not enough, the string's angle will cause the arrow to fly to the left of the target.

This is why the spine of the arrow is critical to correct and accurate shooting. If you are consistently shooting to one side or the other of the target, check the spine of the arrows. Canting the bow will not accommodate the arrow's flight enough to compensate for this. The archer's paradox is not a problem of the bow, as some writers have suggested, but rather a problem of the arrow. Experiment with different arrow spines and see what works best. As with anything else, it takes a practiced and experienced bowyer to match the spine of the arrow to the bow the first time out.

✠ ✠ ✠

No matter what method you choose to shoot,

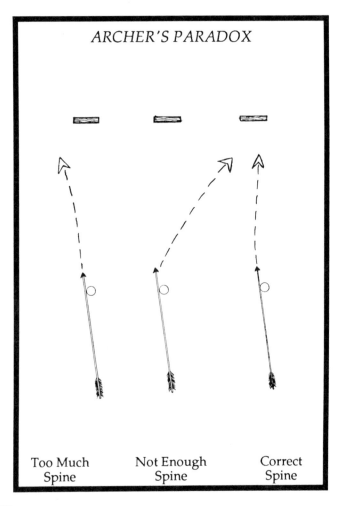

ARCHER'S PARADOX

Too Much Spine   Not Enough Spine   Correct Spine

stand, release and aim, do it because it satisfies you. No one can say their brand of archery is better than your's just because they can hit the bullseye more times or their group is tighter. Modern concepts of marksmanship with both guns or bows are based upon standards set forth by English archers in the fourteenth century, before the Indian even had the bow. There is no dispute that the archers of Europe were unsurpassable when in a firm position, but is hitting a target at one hundred yards in a firm posture more or less difficult than sitting on horseback running full tilt and hitting a buffalo chip at a distance of six feet? I think not. We must realize that there are many types of archery and just as many standards of quality to go with them. You cannot compare the accuracy of the contemporary compound bow with sights, release mechanisms and draw verifiers to the quality and sweetness of the primitive bow. Yes, they both shoot arrows, but you can also get to the mountain top either by helicopter or foot; and, therein lies the difference.

Many times I have sat around a table with friends who are down-grading other forms of archery, speaking of bows with "training wheels," etc. I even participated in these discussions, until one day a student made the comment that archery is archery. There are differences in mechanics, but the thrill one feels as the arrow speeds off and strikes the target, dead center is the same. I still feel there is more challenge in primitive archery, but I no longer feel it is the only form of archery.

✠ ✠ ✠

Do all the modern contrivances allow for more accurate archery? Yes, but for better archery? No. Just different archery. There will be those that make light of the kind of shooting you do. Just smile and refrain from comment. Those who live in the hills may never know more than those who live in the city, but they will always know some things that city people will never fathom.

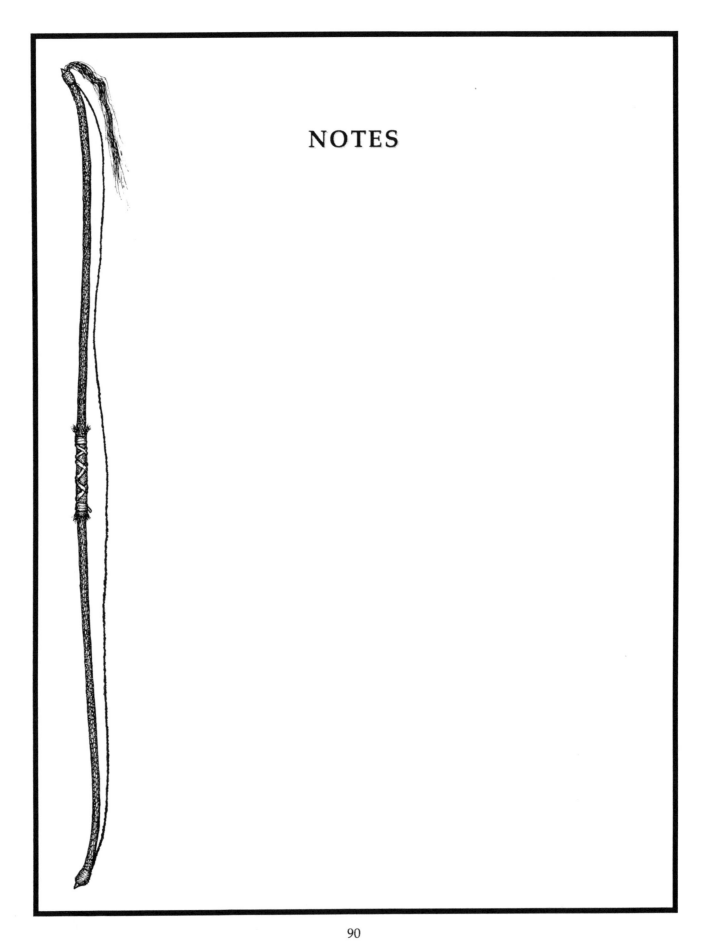

NOTES

GLOSSARY

Archer's Paradox - The arrow bending around the grip and straightening out as the bow string returns to its normal braced height.

Arrow - A straight missile that is launched from the bow.

Arrowsmith - One who makes arrows.

Artillery - The original meaning denoted bows and arrows.

Back - The flat side of the bow that faces away from the shooter; opposite the belly.

Backing - Any material placed on the back of the bow to improve cast, weight or safety.

Belly - The side of the bow that faces the shooter; rounded part of the bow; opposite the back.

Bend - To place the string on the bow.

Bow Stave - The chunk of uncut wood that will become the bow.

Billet - See bow stave.

Bowyer - The maker of bows.

Brace - To bend the bow to take a string; adjusting the string.

Cast - The distance the bow throws the arrow.

Clout - Shooting at a small object placed on the ground at a considerable distance. Sometimes mistakenly referred to as "cloud" shooting due to the manner in which the arrow is fired.

Cock Feather - The feather that is perpendicular to the nock; the feather that faces the outside of the bow when fired.

Compound Bow - A bow that is laminated with two or more layers of the same material; a modern bow consisting of pulleys and cables.

Compression - The belly of the bow undergoes compression or a lateral flattening when the bow is drawn.

Crest - The arrowmaker's or archer's identification mark on the arrow.

Crystal - A crushed segment of fibers or wood cells on the belly; see "follow the string."

Draw - To pull the bowstring back to its proper distance.

Drawfingers - The fingers used to draw the string.

Ears - The tips of the recurve bow.

Eyes - The loops at the ends of the bow-string.

Finger Tabs - A leather protector for the drawfingers.

Fletch - To place the feathers on the arrow shaft.

Fletcher - Arrowsmith.

Flight Arrow - An ultra-light arrow with little fletchings that is used to compare bows or to shoot over great distances.

Follow the String - A bow is following the string when the limbs begin to set in the direction of the bow string; a collapse of the wood cells.

Foreshaft - Some Indian arrows and atlatl darts have a small stick in the end of the shaft. This sometimes holds the arrowhead.

Grip - The handle of the bow.

Head - The object on the front of the arrow.

Instinctive Aim - A method of aiming whereby the shooter is confident that the arrow will strike on target; shooting without aim.

Kick - The jarring recoil found in some bows, particularly the double curve.

Length - The consistent distance the archer is shooting at.

Limbs - This is another name for the arms of the bow on either side of the grip.

Longbow - Any bow over sixty inches in length.

Loose - To release the arrow.

Nocks - The grooves in the end of the arrow which holds the string; the slit in the string end of the arrow.

Nocking Point - The point at which the arrow grasps the bowstring.

Over-Bowed - A bow of a weight that cannot be fully drawn; a bow of too great a weight for the archer; drawing an arrow that is too

91

long for the bow, and not bringing the arrow to a full draw.

Point Blank - When the arrow lies flat on the target at a distance from the bow.

Point of Aim - A method of aim, used extensively by modern archers.

Quiver - A device or bag designed for holding arrows.

Reflexed Bow - A bow that has taken on a definite curve away from the archer when not strung; opposite of following the string.

Recurved Bow - A bow whose tips have been forced back in a direction away from the archer; usually increases arrow speed.

Release - To loose or let go of the arrow.

Riser - Same as grip.

Sapwood - The wood of the tree that is directly under the bark, best used for the back of the bow.

Self Arrow - An arrow of one piece of wood.

Self Bow - A bow that is of one piece of material, with no backing.

Shaft - The arrow stick.

Spine - The amount of give or bend that an arrow has; how it bends around the grip of the bow.

Stacking - The point of undesirable stiffness a bow may reach when approaching full draw.

Tab - See finger tab.

Tension - The back of the bow is stretched to the point of stiffness when drawn; also known as "extension."

Tiller - The art of making the bow bend equally in both limbs.

Turn - Another term for a twist in the bows limbs.

Vane - A feather that is meant for fletching.

Weight - The draw strength of a bow in pounds; the actual weight of the arrow.

BIBLIOGRAPHY AND INDEX

BUREAU OF AMERICAN ETHNOLOGY: Teton Sioux Music, Bulletin 61, 1915.

CONN, Richard: A Persistent Vision, Denver Art Museum, 1986.

DEVOTO, Bernard: Journals of Lewis and Clarke, Houghton/Mifflin, 1953.

ELMER, Robert P.: Target Archery, Private Publishing.

EWING, Douglas: Pleasing the Spirits, Ghylen Press, 1982.

FEDER, Norman: Buffalo and the Indian, Denver Art Museum, 1930.

GRINNELL, George: Cheyenne Indians, Yale Press, 1923.

HAMILTON, T.M.: Native American Bows, Missouri Archeological Society, 1982.

KLOPSTEG, Paul: Turkish Archery and the Composite Bow, Private Publishing, 1947.

LA FLESCHE, Francis: Omaha Bow Makers, Smithsonian Annual Report, 1926.

LAUBIN, Reginald: Native American Archery, University of Oklahoma, 1980.

LOWIE, Robert: Indians of the Plains, University of Nebraska, 1954.

MAILS, Thomas: Mystic Warriors of the Plains, Doubleday, 1972.

POPE, Saxton: Hunting with the Bow and Arrow, Popular Library, 1974.

STEMMLER, L.E.: Archery Workshop, Woods Unusual, 1935.

THOMAS AND RONNEFELDT: People of the First Man, EP Dutton, 1976.

VANGEN, Roland: Indian Weapons, Filter Press, 1972.

WALLENTINE, Douglas: Making Arrows the Old Way, Eagle's View Publishing Company, 1988.

INDEX

SOME EAGLE'S VIEW BESTSELLERS THAT MAY BE OF INTEREST:

❑ Eagle's View Publishing Catalog of Books	B00/00	$4.00
❑ The Technique of Porcupine Quill Decoration/Orchard	B00/01	$9.95
❑ The Technique of North American Indian Beadwork/Smith	B00/02	$13.95
❑ Techniques of Beading Earrings by Deon DeLange	B00/03	$9.95
❑ More Techniques of Beading Earrings by Deon DeLange	B00/04	$9.95
❑ Crow Indian Beadwork/Wildschut and Ewers	B00/06	$10.95
❑ New Adventures in Beading Earrings by Laura Reid	B00/07	$9.95
❑ Traditional Indian Crafts by Monte Smith	B00/10	$9.95
❑ Traditional Indian Bead & Leather Crafts by Smith & VanSickle	B00/11	$9.95
❑ Indian Clothing of the Great Lakes: 1740-1840/Hartman	B00/12	$13.95
❑ Shinin' Trails: A Possibles Bag of Fur Trade Trivia by Legg	B00/13	$8.95
❑ Adventures in Creating Earrings by Laura Reid	B00/14	$9.95
❑ Circle of Power by William Higbie	B00/15	$8.95
❑ Etienne Provost: Man of the Mountains by Jack Tykal	B00/16	$9.95
❑ A Quillwork Companion by Jean Heinbuch	B00/17	$12.95
❑ Making Indian Bows & Arrows...The Old Way by Doug Spotted Eagle	B00/18	$12.95
❑ Making Arrows...The Old Way by Doug Spotted Eagle	B00/19	$4.50
❑ Hair of the Bear: Campfire Yarns & Stories by Eric Bye	B00/20	$9.95
❑ How To Tan Skins The Indian Way by Evard Gibby	B00/21	$4.50
❑ A Beadwork Companion by Jean Heinbuch	B00/22	$12.95
❑ Beads and Cabochons by Patricia Lyman	B00/23	$10.95
❑ Earring Designs by Sig: Book I by Sigrid Wynne-Evans	B00/24	$10.95
❑ Creative Crafts by Marj by Marj Schneider	B00/25	$9.95
❑ How To Bead Earrings by Lori Berry	B00/26	$10.95
❑ Delightful Beaded Earring Designs by Jan Radford	B00/27	$9.95
❑ Earring Designs by Sig: Book II by Sigrid Wynne-Evans	B00/28	$10.95
❑ Voices of Native America: Music/Instruments by Doug Spotted Eagle	B00/29	$17.95
❑ Craft Cord Corral by Janice S. Ackerman	B00/30	$8.95
❑ Hemp Masters: Hip Hemp Jewelry by Max Lunger	B00/31	$13.95
❑ Classic Earring Designs by Nola May	B00/32	$9.95
❑ How To Make Primitive Pottery by Evard Gibby	B00/33	$8.95
❑ Plains Indian & Mountain Man Arts and Crafts by C. Overstreet	B00/34	$13.95
❑ Beaded Images: Intricate Beaded Jewelry by Barbara Elbe	B00/35	$9.95
❑ Earring Designs by Sig-Book III: Celebrations by Sigrid Wynne-Evans	B00/36	$10.95
❑ Techniques of Fashion Earrings by Deon DeLange	B00/37	$9.95
❑ Beaded Images II: Intricate Beaded Jewelry by Barbara Elbe	B00/38	$9.95
❑ Picture Beaded Earrings for Beginners by Starr Steil	B00/39	$9.95
❑ Plains Indian & Mountain Man Arts and Crafts II by C. Overstreet	B00/40	$12.95
❑ Simple Lace and Other Beaded Jewelry Patterns by Mary Ellen Harte	B00/41	$6.95
❑ Beaded Treasure Purses by Deon DeLange	B00/42	$10.95
❑ The Art of Simulating Eagle Feathers by Bob Gutierrez	B00/43	$9.95
❑ Treasury of Beaded Jewelry: Bead Stringing Patterns for All Ages	B00/44	$8.95

EAGLE'S VIEW PUBLISHING READERS SERVICE, DEPT B&A
6756 North Fork Road - Liberty, Utah 84310

Please send me the above title(s). I am enclosing $_____ (Please add $5.50 per order to cover shipping and handling.) Send check or money order - no cash or C.O.D.s.

Ms./Mrs./Mr. _____

Address _____

City/State/Zip Code _____

Prices and availability subject to change without notice. Allow 2 to 4 weeks for delivery.

THE ART OF SIMULATING EAGLE FEATHERS

by
Bob Gutierrez

Another coup for Eagle's View and You!! Nobody else has anything like this fantastic new handbook!! It is the <u>only</u> full color, instructional manual which teaches crafters how to create realistic imitation Golden and Bald Eagle feathers that can be legally used in all of their projects. Noted craftsman and educator Bob Gutierrez shares more than 20 years of experience in creating these marvelous works of art. Explanatory photographs and written descriptions of each and every step required, from feather preparation through each step in the painting process are provided. These same techniques can, of course, be used to create simulations of other predatory species, which are also protected by law. Simple tools, easily obtained materials and a desire to create beauty are all that are needed to get the most out of this book. These feathers are perfect for traditional or contemporary Indian arts and crafts projects and may be created for use in headdresses, bustles, roaches, scalp locks, dream catchers, wall hangings and to decorate almost any project. Don't miss out on this unique book!!

ISBN 0-943604-59-1 in paperback - $9.95

TECHNIQUES OF
BEADING EARRINGS
by
Deon DeLange

This is the exciting book that started a new trend in Native American-style crafts and continues to be a best seller in "how-to" craft books.

Included are complete easy to follow, step-by-step instructions for making earrings and necklaces of all kinds. In addition to the "reader approved" text, there are over thirty-eight plates, examples, charts and illustrations to help the craftsperson create beautiful earrings and matching necklaces. Photographs are presented in black/white and in full color.

Written and explained in clear detail by Deon DeLange, this book features beautiful illustrations by noted graphics artist Monte (Smitty) Smith, Jr., and is a must for any creative person.

ISBN 0-943604-03-6 - $9.95

Also available is Volume II, *More Techniques of Beading Earrings* by *Deon DeLange* that expands upon the concepts introduced in the book noted above. Even more of these exciting styles are explained in step-by-step detail. A fine book.

ISBN 0-943604-12-5 - $9.95

The Techniques of
NORTH AMERICAN
INDIAN BEADWORK
by
Monte Smith

This informative and easy to read book was written by noted author and editor Monte Smith and contains complete instructions on every facet of doing beadwork.

Included in this bestselling craft book are directions for selecting, buying and using beading materials; guidelines for either buying or making your own beadwork loom; and, an examination of Indian beadwork, designs (with a special emphasis on tribal differences), their development, significance and uses.

There are step-by-step instructions for all of the variations of beading techniques used in both loom and applique work and directions for beading round objects, rosettes and necklaces.

This book of 102 pages contains approximately 200 illustrations, examples and photos (some in full color) of beaded articles from 1835 to the present. Photographs of beaded articles include examples from the Apache, Arapaho, Assiniboine, Bannock, Blackfoot, Cheyenne, Chippewa-Cree, Comanche, Cree, Crow, Flathead, Gros Ventre, Huron, Kiowa, Mohawk, Navajo, Ojibwa, Omaha, Otto, Paiute, Pottawatomi, Sac & Fox, Shoshoni, Umatilla, Ute, Winnebago and Yakima.

This exciting book will be of interest to every craftsperson with interests in American Indian beadwork or to anyone who wishes to know more about the material culture of Native Americans.

ISBN 0-943604-02-8 in Paperback - $13.95

AVAILABLE AT DEALERS OR FROM
Eagle's View Publishing Company
6756 North Fork Road
Liberty, Utah 84310
Please include $5.50 per order for Shipping Charges

Also Available:

Eagle's View Publishing Company Catalog of Books & Patterns	$3.50
Eagle Feather Trading Post Annotated Catalog of Books	$4.00
Eagle Feather Trading Post Catalog of Arts & Crafts Supplies	$4.00